This book is a work of fiction. Any references to historical events, real people, or real locales are used factiously. Other names, characters, places, and incidents are the product of the authors imagination, and any resemblance to actual events or locales, or persons, living or dead, is entirely coincidental.

ISBN-13: 978-0-692-79402-9

ISBN-10: 0-692-79402-6

I dedicate this work to my family who have always supported me-- no matter what. I thank God for you all every day.

Breaking Free

Allie Early

PROLOGUE

Crime rates were ravaging America. No one was safe. The prisons were so full that all it took to escape was overpowering the few security guards that were brave enough to stay. That's why President Gerald took action.

He declared that the lower half of California was going to be a dumping ground for prisoners. The evacuation of South California took only two months. That is all the time it took for 13 million people to leave their home. The concrete monster of a wall was built around lower California to corral the nation's worst crime offenders. The wall was built by 1.2 million criminals who had only committed petty crimes and were working off their jail time. Building the Prison Wall (as it was named) only took one month. In the three months following the last slab of concrete being put in place, the government transported every prisoner who had committed high caliber crimes to rot away inside that wall, not to be bothered with again. As I saw all this happening in the news I never, not once, thought I might be going behind it one day....

"I was only following my instinct. He was going to kill me, please, I am innocent!" I pleaded with the officials. Used to, anyone accused of a crime would have the opportunity to go before a judge and let him decide if you were guilty or not. Now, the police decide on site if you will spend the rest of your life in a cage and they are merciless. They found me guilty. I remember that day so vividly because that was the day my life changed forever.

1. Backstory

I spent my entire adolescent life in a small South Carolina town right on the coast of the Atlantic Ocean where the only thing to keep you entertained was sailing on water or walking on sand. My parents and I lived in a four-bedroom house that always smelled of lavender because of the lavender plants my mother grew in every window sill. The kitchen was on the small side and did not get used much on account that my mother could burn water. Most of the time the whole house felt like a cage. My room was the only place I did not feel completely cornered. It was the only bedroom with a working fireplace and on cold nights' silver moonlight would bounce off my forest green walls, mingling with the orange glow of firelight. I would stay up for hours surrounded by that mixture of light, reading books about people who had adventures in far off lands and imagining what it would be like if I were one of the book characters.

Even though most of the time I felt trapped in that small town, I had a wonderful life with two caring parents. My father was a large man with a stern face, framed by chin-length brown hair. He did not smile much, and on the rare occasions he did, it seemed to take him a lot of energy to lift the corners of his mouth upward. Although some may describe him as dull, my father was anything but boring. Every weekend he would take me sailing, and we would fish for hours. Sometimes we'd talk about everything and sometimes we'd only listen to the lapping of the waves. Over years of our weekly voyages, I started to feel like an extension of the ocean itself.

My mother was the opposite of my father. She had a small frame but a big personality with spontaneity as her core trait. I remember her always laughing, and everyone she met instantly fell in love with her. And while both of my parents were wonderful people, they were way too overprotective and quickly became suffocating to my independent teenage self.

As I became a teenager, their constant questioning and desire to be in my life every second bothered me. I felt like I was always under a microscope and the town was the petri dish I was trapped under. Now, I long for my parents, and I even miss the quiet comfort of knowing every square inch of my hometown. However, this realization didn't occur to me when I was a self-righteous 18-year-old boy ready to do whatever it took to escape.

As it happened, my escape hatch came in the form of a scholarship to the University of South Carolina. My plan had always been pretty typical; go to college, get a degree, meet a girl, marry, get a job, then just live. My life did not turn out like this. Sometimes I try to think what I could have done differently so that my life would've ended up like that, but what is the use in doing that? Life has become a rare commodity for me, and I do not care to waste it thinking "what if's" and "could have been."

I ended up graduating with a degree in technological language and no life experience. The day I graduated, the realization hit that the past four years had not held any kinds of stories like in the adventure books I used to read within the four walls of my room. To remedy this, I decided to see what the world was like outside the confines of South Carolina before I tied myself down to a career.

Before I set off into the unknown, my parents drove me back to their house which to my surprise was overflowing with the townspeople I had known my whole life. It was a bit embarrassing that such a fuss was made with me in the spotlight, but someone graduating college was a rare occurrence in that small town, and it required recognition. Later that night, the front door finally closed on the last homemade casserole. I was left with the feeling of relief, but also a sense of something ending. I remember saying goodnight to my parents then retreating to my room. I flipped through all the books that had comforted me with the promise there was more in the world than what I had known. The next morning, I said a forever goodbye to the small town that raised me.

As my town became smaller and smaller in my car's rearview mirror, a feeling of panic hit me. I had no idea where to go or what the next chapter of my life held. I felt that fear only for a minute or two then panic melted into excitement. I had no idea where to go or what was next in my life! I wanted to see everything, experience everything. I wanted to see Britain, Germany, Russia, all the places my books described to me. Unfortunately, a decade ago the United States banned international travel due to the epidemic that had destroyed half the population of Europe, Russia, and two-thirds the population of Africa. For a time, everyone thought the human race would be obliterated. When the pandemonium in America reached its height, the government stopped all air travel, even within the country, and put the supposed infected people in quarantine. One year later, they opened the airports again, but only travel within the U.S. was allowed. Even still, I was happy as a lark simply because I was finally escaping the borders of South Carolina.

2. Saved My Life

I traveled nonstop for months. Living out of my suitcase, meeting interesting people, basically fulfilling my childhood dream, but no matter how many new places I saw or how many new people I met, something was missing. When I reached my wit's end, I was twenty-one and had no idea what I needed to feel whole. I was so naive and lost that I decided I didn't want to be on this Earth anymore. Florida was one of the best places I had visited on my travels so I thought it'd be a good of a place as any to die, so I traveled south to Tallahassee, Florida. The deal I made with myself was that if I hadn't changed my mind after one week, I'd buy some pills and end my suffering the cowardly way.

I stayed on the beach for six days. I slept there,

walked on the shore, and watched the fiery sunset every day but I still felt empty. On the seventh day, I stopped in a nutrient store to buy my 'cure.' I distinctly remember reaching out to grab the last bottle of death the store had, but someone else's hand was quicker than mine. I sheepishly drew my hand away and apologized to the older man with peppered gray hair, kind green eyes, and a small frame. I immediately got the sense that he was a grandfather. He laughed so warmly it reminded me of a fire crackling. "It's alright son; I just need these for my back. My wife told me not to go sailing yesterday, and she's always right," he said while bringing his hand to his mouth like he was telling me a secret.

Even in my depressed state, I found myself laughing. "Well, I hope they help." In my mind, I hoped he would only say thank you and walk away so I could find some other pills that would finish my suffering. Thankfully, he didn't leave me. Looking back at this memory, I suspect that he knew what I was going through.

"Well, listen, let me buy you some food, and in exchange, you can keep me company for lunch." I looked at him uncertainly, but being a twenty-three-year-old, free food was an offer I could not resist. After he had purchased our lunches, we found a small table right outside the nutrient store. "So what is your story, sonny?" he asked me.

"Well, my name is Justin Price, and I recently graduated from college. Now I am taking some time to travel." He looked at me with curiosity, and I immediately knew he was one of those rare souls that accepted people for who they are and loved them no matter what. We talked for hours. I discovered he was a pastor for a Baptist church, a short walking distance from where we sat. We discussed sailing, the epidemic, and then I surprised myself by telling him about the pain and emptiness I had been feeling. He just nodded his head and listened to my hurting without judgment. Now I know that something as simple as him caring enough to listen had pulled me from the edge of a cliff that I would've never climbed back up. After two hours of conversation, Pastor Barrios, as he was known, asked me where I was staying. When I told him, I had not thought that far ahead, he offered to loan me out one of his church's rooms to stay in. The only condition

11

was I had to come to his Sunday service. I accepted and, honestly, it was a decision that saved my life.

That Sunday everyone I met was so kind and welcoming and when they sang the entire room felt physically charged with power. I had never felt anything like it. My parents were never very religious, but I had friends that were believers. I had never really understood the point of praying to some unknown entity. That Sunday, I discovered prayer was only a small part of believing. Christianity was much more complicated. I stayed in Florida to learn more about God and faith. With each day, I began to feel a sense of purpose, along with an overwhelming feeling that there might be a heaven and someone who could take away all my worries and pain without the detrimental effects of drugs. Two months later, I decided to be reborn in Christ. This event was a turning point in my young life because it gave me the fulfillment I needed to move on from a life of searching and begin using my life to help people.

With my new faith giving me strength, I asked Pastor Barrios to help me find a job. He put me in touch with a friend of his that worked for a government organization in Baltimore, Maryland, where the streets were littered with drugs and broken people. I knew that I could help those people by doing the same thing Pastor Barrios did for me; I would listen. I called his friend and got a job at the government agency designed to improve livability in cities worst affected by the increase in criminal activity. Baltimore had the highest percentage of prisoners sent behind the wall, and I wanted to help change that. I said goodbye to the people who had become my family and headed off to save the world, with God's help of course.

I soon discovered that saving the world was harder than I thought. On a day to day basis, I would work in front of the holographic screens, analyzing arrest reports and trying to find patterns that would explain why people were turning to violence. Now and then I was allowed to go out in the safer parts of the city to talk to residents, collect suggestions, and assess living conditions to see if any improvements were being made.

On a warm, but cloudy evening, I decided to ask my boss for one of these expeditions. At that point, I hadn't been out in the field for over a month, and I was tired of sitting in my desk chair staring at data. I left my tiny box of an office to set up the mission with my supervisor. He gave me the okay along with the access key to the defense room. Just as I was headed out his office door he said, "Price, make sure to take a guard robot because the prison across town had some escaped inmates they're searching for." I nodded only half listening to him. I was simply relieved that he said I could go. I quickly walked through the cold, sterile hallway to the defense room.

I only vaguely remember what the Defense Room was like mostly because it was always so dimly lit. In truth, it was more of a warehouse building than a room. There was floor to ceiling metal shelves that lined the walls and in the back was where the guard robots "lived." Those machines were top of the line, technology wise, and reached the height of my chin. Their domed shaped bodies could slide open on command to reveal multiple weapons. The agency had bought them a year before I began work there. They were designed to protect our agents at all costs. At the time, I was a very proud guy who told himself that if I went into the field with one of these hulking robots at my side, the public would refuse to answer my

questions from fear of the frightening metal guards.

In result of that weak logic, and against my boss's advice, I went without the guard robots and just brought a small revolver. I confidently walked out of the office because at age twenty-three I had not yet discovered that I wasn't invincible.

3. Hostage Situation

I have always loved to drive, especially in my younger days. Being behind the wheel gave me a sense of complete control. There was something so freeing about driving with the radio on and the windows down. It was almost as if I were a bird how the wind whipped my hair around as I flew past houses and street signs getting closer to my destination. My first car was a solar-plex emota. A great car that was solely run off solar power. When I was sixteen, "green" cars were all the rage, and they still are. However, they aren't as big of a deal now because of a law passed by the government's environmental branch, making it illegal to buy or sell a new car that ran off gas because those cars polluted the environment. All cars now have to be electric or solar powered, and since every car is legally required to have a "green" stamp of approval, the excitement over the solar technology quickly faded into normalcy.

The day my life changed course, I drove the company's government issued car with its autopilot feature off so that I could be in control. Big mistake.

I thought I knew what roads to drive down, but I took all the wrong turns. I ended up in a desolate neighborhood where ivy had taken over the walls and ink black darkness was in the place of where the buildings' doors and windows should be. I immediately turned on the autopilot and tried to turn around, but it was too late.

As soon as the car righted its direction I was faced with a gang of three rough looking guys. I immediately knew they were prisoners because of their red arm tattoo that brands every convicted criminal with an assigned number based on the date and time of their arrest. Often the criminals that escaped prison would come to abandoned places, such as this neighborhood because they knew no one is dumb enough to come close. Well, no one except me, and the official government vehicle I was

17

sitting in didn't help my situation. I reached into my pocket and felt the small revolver, which at this point was more of a psychological comfort than an actual help to my situation.

"Get outta' the car with your hands up," shouted the lithe leader of the small group. I sat in my car paralyzed by fear; a million thoughts were racing through my head, so much adrenaline pumping through my veins I could see my skin pulse along with my heartbeat. Every second felt like a century. As they stared at me, I tried to think of an exit. Eventually, the stalemate was over, and the largest of the three guys came at the car door lock with an old rusty hammer. I know it's stupid but all I could think at that moment was I wonder who's hammer that used to be.

The hammer hit the lock three times, and with that last thud, the only barrier between them and me was ripped away. Two of the guys threw me out of the car. The pavement felt gritty as the left side of my body scraped across the ground. I remember them asking who I was, what I was doing, and a bunch of other questions along that line. I think I answered them, but I could barely hear any sound other than the rapid thumping of my heartbeat.

"Let's jus' kill em' Ronnie," the giant who broke the door lock said to the leader. The guy was at least six-three and spoke with a thick southern accent. His greasy and matted blonde hair showed that his primary concern certainly wasn't hygiene.

I knew it would have been useless to run. Even though I didn't see any guns on them, they probably knew this neighborhood better than I ever would. Also, not to mention the fact that for every three strides I took, the tall hammer guy made one. I'd never outrun them, and then they would kill me immediately. My adrenaline jumbled brain wasn't much help in thinking of a solution, and so while the prisoners were tossing around ideas of what they should do with me, I closed my eyes and prayed. I prayed that God would give me a way, an idea, anything to escape my impending death. My mind cleared, and one thought persisted. When I opened my eyes, a sharp, glinting knife was coming toward my throat.

"Wait! You don't want to kill me!" I screamed. The hand wielding the knife froze one foot away from slicing my neck open. The feeling I felt at this moment brings up a picture of the Greek mythological sisters called the Fates hovering my life string in between their scissors. The only plan that my brain could configure was to convince them that they would benefit from holding me hostage.

I lied to them by shakily saying "I am a very important government leader. If you kill me, you will spend the rest of your lives living a fate worse than death. If you hold me hostage, you can barter your safe passage to Canada. I would get to keep my life and so would each of you. It's a win-win."

First off, I was not an important anybody. Second, no one ever would be granted safe passage to Canada. It wouldn't even matter if you were holding President Gerald himself hostage! However, they didn't know these two details. The knife was put in the third prisoner's back pocket, and my life was spared for the time being. I breathed a sigh of relief as they dragged me to my feet and pushed me forward. It felt like my feet were anchors, the only positive thing in that situation was they forgot to check my pockets.

I still had my pistol. The only tool I could use

against these three hit heavily against my thigh with each step I took. I thought to myself, maybe when they go to sleep, I could sneak away, and if they woke up, I could use my revolver. The measly scrap of a plan probably had a one in a million chance of actually getting me out of this alive, but it would have to work.

4. Self-Defense

We walked about three blocks to probably the only house in the neighborhood that still had a front door and a few intact window panels. I looked to the sky and by the position of the sun I guessed the time to be 19:00. My parents used to tell me when they were young; military time wasn't used, but a few years before I was born, every country agreed to centralize measurement systems, such as time, temperature, and distances. I often long for my parent's stories of old the old days, and as I walked through that abandoned house's doorway, I remember badly wanting to be in a dream where I would soon wake up to the smell of lavender instead of musty mildew.

Unfortunately, I was not dreaming, and my situation was in fact very real. Immediately entering the house, I felt an enormous pressure hit the back of my head. I blacked out. When I gained consciousness, I found myself slumped against the living room wall trying to ignore how much the back of my head throbbed. All three prisoners were huddled around the kitchen bar whispering urgently. Ronnie, the leader, was the first to notice I had come back to the land of the living. I slowly felt for my revolver; I still had it.

"Well, well, well, look who's finally awake!" Ronnie's mocking laughter rang through the chilled house, "Edgar, you and Sal head out to raid that convenience store uptown that sells the pills and grab some food. They won't call the cops. The last thing they need is a bunch of officials snooping around their merchandise. It's dark enough now where anyone who's out won't want any trouble, especially in this part of the city. I'll stay here and watch our golden goose," he winked in my direction as he twirled a 5-inch razor blade between his long spindly fingers. Although my situation was not ideal, my ears perked up when I heard that two of the guys would be leaving. One criminal instead of three gave me much better odds of escaping. This turn of events lifted my spirits and took the edge off the pain I felt from the lump that had formed on the back of my head.

Edgar and Sal left a few minutes later, and Ronnie sat in the kitchen reading a book that was falling apart. I waited at least fifteen minutes before preparing myself to kill this man to prevent him from killing me when he found out I was useless. By the twenty-minute mark, I figured I'd allowed enough time for the two prisoners to get out of ear range before I did anything crazy.

Ronnie had his back to me, and I slowly reached for my revolver. A memory of the first time I had ever shot a gun surfaced from the back of my mind. Surrounded by shadows of massive trees in a forest right outside town, my dad told me to pick a tree and aim. Then, I'd just have to pull the trigger. For survival purposes, Dad wanted me to have the experience of shooting a gun. I was seven years old, and crimes rates were sky high, the epidemic was just beginning and every source of news screamed that the world was going to end.

Ronnie started to cough, jerking my mind back into the dank interior of the abandoned house. I had a gun in my hand now. I remember so vividly the same feeling of that gun in my hand when I was seven. I closed my eyes for a second and imagined I was back in the forest swallowed up by fresh air and the safe cover of trees. My seven-year-old-self aimed at a tree, pulling the trigger back making a grating *chtick*. The explosion of noise hit my ears and rattled my bones. Suddenly I was not a kid in a forest, and the bleeding figure in front of me was not a tree. Ronnie's body jerked and flailed. His eyes locked on to mine full of pain and hatred. As long as I live, that look of pure hate will forever be burned into my memory. Eventually, he became rigid, and his hating eyes glazed over. Even though the house was cold enough to make my fingers feel like ice, I broke into a sweat.

The explosion echoed through the city walls, bouncing off the buildings like a pinball game. A pool of red blood seeped from Ronnie's body onto the floor like a rain puddle. The shock of taking a human life is too immense to describe. I remember every detail of the scene. The old book Ronnie was reading lay on the floor, slowly absorbing the warm blood flowing from its owner. How the ugly floral wallpaper was peeling from the wall. How the wood flooring creaked from under me and the look of the open dead eyes of a human with no soul behind them. I turned and ran out the front door into the dark night.

5. Turning Point

I blindly ran for what felt like hours until I finally collapsed in an alley behind a rusted dumpster. Jumping at every sound, cringing from the biting chill, and wishing I was back in my cozy apartment eating mac and cheese was, at the time, one of the worst feelings I'd experienced in my short life. Sound, sight, touch, every sense felt heightened. My mind raced, I could not relax or decide what to do next. So I sat and waited. I didn't have a sense of time. I could have been sitting there for hours or days. It didn't matter. When the sun began peeking over the buildings, I walked toward it. East was the direction of home.

I started to wonder if anyone at work would miss me or wonder where I was if I was safe. I didn't have a girlfriend or friends for that matter. I hadn't called my parents since I had left home and I wasn't close with my coworkers except for the occasional hello when passing in the hallway. The moment I realized that I had no one who would miss me, I vowed to make at least one friend when I got back home. Sadly, I never got the chance.

The flashing lights and sirens came on me so fast they encompassed my whole being. The noise was so consuming it seemed like the blue lights, and deafening noise made up the very air I breathed. For the second time in two days, my body was forced onto the concrete streets. I tried to explain to the police officials what I had been through, but I was only answered by "shut-ups" and "anything you say will be held against you." The hand chains they slapped on my wrist felt like they weighed twenty-five pounds, probably because I had no strength due to not eating or hydrating for at least twenty-four hours.

Gravel dug into my forehead like a drill into wood. I couldn't see how many officials were surrounding me, but I registered at least four voices. My heart and lungs hurt as they worked overtime from the adrenaline that was once again pumping through my veins. I was scared. The police were smarter than the escaped criminals in that they checked my pockets immediately. My throat tightened, why did I never throw the gun away?

"What have you got here buddy?" an official said to me while handing the gun to his partner. I couldn't speak as the tightening in my throat worsened. My vocal cords were twisted so tightly I feared they would break under the pressure.

"Looks like it's the same caliber gun that killed that escapee Ronnie Miller that we discovered earlier today on Toulouse Street. Let's run the ballistics to see if we have a match." I knew as soon as that fact became verified, my life would be over. They asked me a few more questions that I cannot recall, but it didn't matter what questions I answered because in their eyes I had committed a murder, period. No self-defense ruling or concrete evidence was needed for those officials to throw me into the back of their black as death patrol cars, lock the door and declare me guilty. How did they sleep at night? Why were they so eager to destroy my life? They were like guard robots with their lack of emotional connection. I pleaded, begged, cried, screamed over and over again, "I was only following my instinct. He was going to kill me, please listen, I am innocent!" Their ears may have registered my screams but all their brains perceived was, "He is guilty. He is guilty. He must be locked away forever."

The car began to move forward, taking me away to rot in a cage; leaving my freedom to wither away on the concrete sidewalks of Baltimore.

6. Corruption

Here in the back of this police car, I remember those events that led up to me sitting here, surrounded by locked doors. I am like a captured bird. I try to look outside as the car flies past neighborhoods, stores, unattainable freedom, but the windows are blacked out and instead I am forced to observe my beat up black and white sneakers.

The vehicle jerks to a stop and the passenger side door opens, pouring in bright sunlight that burns my eyes. The official who first slapped the cuffs on my wrists now pulls me from the car and holds a gun to my back, pushing me forward. As my eyes adjust, a gray cinder block building comes into focus. With sky-high electric fences surrounding the place, even the sunshine looks dreary. I am terrified to find out what lies behind the walls of this place.

The official presents his identification, and we are hurried inside the prison. I am met with a waiting area, where family and friends of criminals used to sit and wait for a chance to see their loved ones. Now, instead of kind people innocently waiting, the chairs are occupied by prisoners who are all handcuffed to their seat's elbow rest. I am so confused. Are these criminals waiting to get placed in jail too?

Their arm tattoos burn bright red, the color of blood. I do not understand why these criminals are here or why the official is typing something into a keyboard. I find myself being forced to sit beside one of the seated prisoners. He was an older dark skinned man with a toothless mouth. Still confused, I squirm to the edge of my seat only for the toothless prisoner to grab my hand and saddle the underside of my left forearm with a sticky black pad. I look into his brown eyes to find sadness and pity. His eyes squeeze shut as his arthritic finger presses a black button on the pad. Immediately following, a thousand tiny needles gorge into my flesh. My brain enters panic mode, and I scream out in pain. The officials in the room hoarsely chuckle and the five or six prisoners also in charge of administering this unbearable pain look on, surely remembering their own suffering. I felt each needle sliding out of my tender skin leaving behind a burning sensation that I don't think will heal anytime soon. The toothless old man ripped off the pad like a band aid. I scream again, gripping my shaking wrist. He quickly smears a clear film across my wound. Hesitantly, my eyes look at the site of my pain. Behind the film, a bright red tattoo stares back at me. My number is 1131300, today's date and the time I was arrested. I assume this information is what the official had typed in before permanently branding me as a criminal.

As my new scar begins going numb from the film, I am pushed toward another door that, I am guessing, leads to my fellow inmates. Now, I am even more terrified than I was outside. Most of these criminals are murderers with no regret and I was an innocent twenty-three-year-old guy who smelled of fear. An official decorated with artillery weapons opens a heavy metal door that leads into a stark white indoor courtyard with tables and prisoners scattered throughout the space. This prison is not very crowded which can only mean they have already shipped most of the criminals out to California; behind the wall.

I quivered as the one hundred pairs of eyes locked onto me. The official continues to push me toward a cell on the outskirts of the courtyard.

"Better try and get some shut eye. We are shipping the last of you murderers behind the wall first thing tomorrow," I cringe as he said the word murderer. I was not a criminal. I did nothing but prevent my own death, and if that is a crime, then half of the officials running this prison should be in this cell. He shut the door with a thud and turned the lock with a bronze key. I didn't understand why he locked me in. Surely it wasn't to keep me safe. I was going to be shipped off to California tomorrow where no one here would ever know, or care if I lived or died.

After an hour or two of staring at the cinderblock wall, I begin to vaguely remember an article I had read that would explain why I was mercilessly arrested, then locked away for safe keeping. Apparently, when the wall was ready to accept its first victims, many prisons did not want to send off their criminals because the government paid a higher dollar amount to higher capacity prisons. To remedy this reluctance, the government decided to stop paying the prisons by how many people they hold at one time, and instead, pay by how many criminals they transport to California. I guess this very change is what lead to my hasty arrest. The more people they could find to send behind the wall, the more money they'd receive.

It dawned on me that the reason the officials arrested me because they were greedy and selfish people who cared more about money than my life. That also must be the reason they locked me in an individual cell. They could not have one of their prime beef cows killed right before they ship their herd off to the slaughter house.

7. A Friend

I lie awake exhausted; unable to stop my brain from creating scenario after scenario of how I will die. Between these horrific scenes, I pray that God would protect me and somehow deliver me to freedom. Eventually, I entered that quirky state of sleep where you're conscious of your worries, but you're somehow also asleep.

I am not sure what time I was brought back to being fully awake. There are no windows to see whether the sun ever came back up again. I jump as an official yanks open the door with a gun pointing at my face. This official is young and obviously inexperienced. He's probably the same age as me. His voice shakes as he says, "Get up and do exactly what I tell you." I slowly put my feet on the ground, weakly placing my body weight on unsteady legs, never breaking eye contact with him. I guess this is the beginning of preparing their cattle for shipment.

With the young officer's gun pointed at my back, I walk toward the cluttered kitchen where at least twenty men are lined up, each chained by their ankles to one another. I became the twenty-first chain link.

We each were given a brown sack with our breakfast inside. An official with fat rolls for a neck and permanently red cheeks screamed at the top of his lungs like an army sergeant, "Do not eat one crumb until you are in the transport vehicle. You will be taken by van to the bullet tram where scum like you all are being taken to California. Once you are on that tram, say goodbye to the real world boys because you ain't comin' back." His words echo off the white walls of the prison and penetrate my heart with terror.

The men in front of me pile into the prison van, my ankle is being pulled by the chains that link us together. I have to follow. Gazing up, I take a long glimpse of the sky, then step inside. The vehicle holds all twenty-one of us and could have easily held twenty more. There are no windows. The only light in the steel interior is three can lights in the ceiling. As I stumble up the steps, a greasy old driver sits behind the wheel. One of his black eyes squints at me while the other looks upward. His face is framed with the few strings of gray hair still attached to his scalp.

I sit beside an older guy. He gives me a weak smile, and I notice his face could have only become that wrinkly from laughing a lot. I give him a sidelined smile as I tear into my food sack like a starving wolf since I haven't seen food or hydration in two days. There isn't much to eat, though. Just an orange, cold sausage meat, half a loaf of bread, and a bag of later. Three days ago I would not have even considered putting this disgusting stuff anywhere near my mouth. Today, I see it as salvation. I finish it all in less than a minute while my seat companion only looks at his. Sheepishly I ask, "Are you going to eat any of that?"

His head turns to me with pity in his face, "No, there is no point in eating when I will be dead tomorrow," he says while dropping the food in my lap. I threw his meal down my throat as well.

"Do you mind me asking how old you are, son?" He asks more like it's a suggestion rather than a question. I decide to tell him a minimal amount about myself, "I am twenty-three, and my name is Justin Price." He nods his head once and sticks out his hand in greeting.

"My name's John, but most people call me Jay." I shake his hand, and we were instantly friends of circumstance. He proceeds to tell me about his life before he was arrested, "Two years ago, I worked at a fishery in Bangor, Maine. Every day smelled of slimy fish guts, but at least I got paid. My job was to organize all the fishnets," Jay smirks at a memory, "They were so heavy I had to use a pulley system just to lift them. One time a guy was helping me out, and the net fell on him. It took a bunch of people to get him out. I'll bet he still has a limp, but I digress."

"I've never even seen a fishery. Did you live close to it?" I ask, surprisingly curious about what his life was like before the chains of jail.

"I actually did live pretty close. I stayed in this little sardine can of an apartment where the rent was cheap, and it was walking distance to the fishery from there. You know, every morning I walked to work about the same time the sun began to peek over the horizon. There's this feeling you get when those sun rays hit your face. Like everything will be alright, yesterday's pain was dulled by the stars and moon. Tomorrow's pain is scared away by the new day sun, and for that moment, just that one moment, the warmth moves through your body and lets you forget any pain or sadness because all you can do is enjoy that very feeling where everything is warm and light." Jay pauses as if he imagined how good it'd be to feel that again.

I nod slowly. I know exactly the feeling he just described. I used to feel it every time I went sailing in my family's small boat. I look down at my feet when the realization that I would probably never sail again hit me like a ton of bricks.

"Anyway, that job and the guys I worked with were pretty much my entire life, as sad as that sounds. You see, my wife had died in a car accident one year before I started working there. She was my entire life. After she died, I had some, uh, dark times. Something happened one night, and I just up and decided it was time to move on" Jay paused but didn't elaborate and I didn't push him.

"Next day, I moved out of the house Meredith and I had shared, and found a job at the fishery. Over the months the job began to fill a bit of the hole in my heart. Of course, a stinky dock only dulled the pain of losing my Meredith, but at least I could function."

Jay looks down at his hands and I wonder what his Meredith was like to make him miss her so much. So I ask him, "What was Meredith like if you don't mind me asking?"

He replied with a wistful smile. "Oh she was beautiful and, like wine, she became even more beautiful with age. Gosh, I miss her laugh, her smile. She had the biggest smile you've ever seen. Her hair was the color of a blackbird, and she had gorgeous green eyes that looked through me like no one ever had." Jay's eyes start to glisten with tears. "We had a daughter named Katy, but she is all grown up now with a family of her own; living down south in Georgia. How about you son? Do you have a lost love?"

"Actually I have never been in love. I guess I just never found any girl who I feel a real connection with." I say a this with a shrug. It's not that I haven't wanted a girlfriend, but dating in my mind ends up with either marriage or heartbreak so you might as well wait until you find someone worthwhile. Of course, now I probably won't ever find anyone because I'll spend the rest of my days surrounded by criminals. Looking around the bus at these intimidating inmates, "the rest of my life" may be cut to a very short amount.

"Jay, how did you get arrested?" I ask him, surprising myself with my boldness. I guess impending doom causes me to be blunter than in typical situations. He sighs, "Well, son, I beat someone to death." I sit in shock. I could not imagine this kind old guy even hurting a fly. He accepts my shock with a sad nod then continues, "Remember how I said that after Meredith passed, I had some dark days and something happened? Most of those days I was completely wasted, and nothing good ever comes from alcohol. One night I sat in a bar drinking the strongest thing they could pour. Obviously, everything I can recall from that night is a bit blurred, but I remember this guy walked in and sat right beside me. He started badgering me about how he needed my seat for a girl he

42

was meeting, even though there were plenty of seats open on the other side of him. I got fed up with his pestering, so I punched him square in the face. He hit me back, and the fight spiraled down from there. I was so angry at the world that took Meredith. I was so angry at this annoying guy. I guess all my emotions that I had been drowning in alcohol finally exploded. The second this poor guy stopped breathing I ran out of the bar. Honestly, I barely stopped running until I reached Bangor. I felt safe in Bangor and decided to sober up, get back on my feet. I haven't had a drink since that night in the bar." Jay's face was full of guilt and regret, "A week after I got to Bangor, I had found a job at the fishery and that small apartment. I was doing well for the first time in a while. I was racked with guilt, of course, but I was at least functioning again. That is, until a month and a day after the murder, some officials caught up to me. They raided my apartment and took me to a prison. Eventually, I was transferred to the one in Maryland."

I know it was hard for him to have relived that experience, "Thanks for telling me all that." I felt like I needed at least one person to know my story too so I ask him if he wants me to share it. He nods and looked at me through curious eyes.

I begin the story when I left my small hometown then ended it with my arrest. Jay opens his mouth and starts to say something, but never got the chance to finish.

8. Bullet Tram

The ancient transport bus comes to an abrupt halt, causing every guy in the bus to hit their heads on the seat in front of them. The door of the bus creaks open ushering in a tiny man with round glasses and a pot belly. Surprisingly, his voice is very deep. Jay leans in and whispers, "His voice reminds me of thunder rumbling." I nod and uneasily think to myself that thunder usually means a storm is coming.

In his rumbling voice, the little man viciously addresses the bus's occupants, "Welcome to the bullet tram station! I hope you got to know your fellow scum on the ride over because from here until you're set loose behind the wall, they will be your traveling mates. Throughout your journey, the chains around your ankles will remain there, and you will follow every single order given to you."

"And if we don't?" One of my "fellow scum," as the tiny man put it, yelled out from the back of the bus.

With a cold gaze, the little man states, "And if you don't follow orders, every bone in your leg will be broken, and you'll live with that pain till you arrive at your final destination on the east coast."

Every one of my fellow bus riders slowly shuffles outside like drunken sailors whose beloved alcohol is unwillingly being left behind in their seats. The tiny man is standing by the door, counting us as our feet move from the last step and onto the ground. Once again I feel like cattle being shipped for slaughter. After the long bus ride, my eyes squint as I try to get accustomed to the sun. For a moment, everything is dazed in a brilliant white light. As the sun's light begins to dull, I find myself wishing I was blinded again. Hundreds of hunched over prisoners are walking toward the old bricked tram station. Some look as scared as I feel and some don't look like they have any emotion at all. A tremble overtakes my body, and my very heart feels as if it may vibrate out of my chest and onto the dirt walkway. I shouldn't even be here, and all I can do is whisper, "God help me."

Stepping inside the station through old metal doors, seeing the exposed brick walls and worn tile floors where so many feet have walked, makes me feel like I am living in a different time period. This station looks exactly like a holograph I learned about in the history class I took a few years ago. A few decades ago, the fastest way to travel across cities was to ride these really trains called subways. Now, instead of the bulky trains that I remember in the holograph, sleek metal tubes sit on the electromagnetic railways.

Jay is walking in front of me, and with every step, the chain linking us twenty-one people creates a thud that seems to echo off the skylights and chipped walls. Officials are everywhere, their eyes follow every group of chained criminals with a disdainful gaze. These officials are in a uniform I've never seen before. Their silver suits, with shiny guns holstered to the side, match the look of the bullet tram.

We eventually weave our way through the mass

crowd of soon-to-be deported prisoners and reach a gate ten feet away from one tram's open compartment. An official begins speaking to the tiny man at the head of our group. Since I am the last person in line, I can't hear what they are saying, but I assume by their hand gestures we are about to board the tram. The official waves us by, and we start to load into the open compartment.

Once inside, I take stock of my surroundings with a sweeping glance. There are no seats on board, only the small expanse of linoleum flooring. All twenty-one of us were crammed in, elbow to elbow. The tiny man yells above the chattering noises of the station, "Good riddance boys. You'll be traveling in this compartment for one day before you are finally in your rightful prison behind the wall." With that, his pot belly turns around and walks out of the compartment. The door slides closed behind him. His words begin to register in my mind. I haven't even thought about what will happen to me after we are dropped behind the wall; carelessly thrown into an abyss of dangerous predators just waiting for some easy prey like me to be thrown inside.

I look over at Jay, and he seems perfectly calm,

while my nerves are running rampant, surrounding me with an inescapable bubble of panic. I decide to calm myself down by focusing on the fact I have never been in a tram. That's because, in the world that I am no longer a part of, only the filthy rich receive the privilege to ride on bullet trams, everyone else uses cars or planes to travel. I am assuming wealthy friends of the government donated these bullet trams as prison transport so that the government would repay their wonderful "generosity" by passing laws to support the upper class' agenda. I get annoyed just thinking about it, so I start to look around.

I notice the guy to my right quickly brushing away tears that rolled down his cheeks like raindrops. I can tell he doesn't want anyone to see him as weak. Everyone else is sitting on the border of the small compartment. Not one of the twenty-one people speak. I look around at the hardened faces that remind me of stone statues, permanently carved with a twisted and pained look. We sit like this for twenty-four hours; no one speaks, no one looks up. The only times there is movement in this small space is when one of us has to relieve ourselves in the hole to the back of the compartment. Every guy has to move toward the hole each time someone has to go because we are all still chained together. And yes, there is literally a hole cut straight through to the tram tracks that we are speeding past.

The only times there is a sound other than the hum of the tram is the chewing of food after meager nutrient packets are sent through a chute in the front of the compartment. I don't know why everyone feels the need to be silent. It is as if the tram has cast a spell forbidding our vocal cords to vibrate. The deafening silence is driving me crazy; every minute feels like an hour and every hour feels like a day.

Just as I felt this tram ride would go on for eternity, a strange sensation of stillness overcame the compartment. I look out the thin window close to the ceiling and notice the greenery of trees. We made it! I know I should not be happy about arriving at the wall, but for the time being, I am just so thankful to be getting out of this small compartment.

I am sitting right across from the door, and as it slides open, the first thing I see is a large rifle carried by a silver uniformed official. "Stand up and start a single file line while coming outside." The official's gun points toward the cloudy gray sky as each of my fellow prisoners spill out of the tram. After being cooped up for one day, my legs feel like bendable straws. As soon as I am able to lock my knees, they collapse from under me, and my hands hit the ground to catch me. Suddenly, a brute force causes me to scream in agony as the official's black shoe connects with my abdomen. "Get up!" He screams again, this time thrusting his gun's barrel into the nap of my neck, "Get up, or I'll shoot you like the worthless piece of garbage you are!" I scramble to my feet, swaying with a head rush that leaves me light headed. I don't deserve being called garbage or scum. I am not a murderer. If I hadn't killed Ronnie, I would be dead, and he would still be on the run. Heck, I did the world a favor.

Jay stumbles in front of me. Up ahead I see a row of prisoners sitting on the ground chained to concrete posts. They reminded me of the people in charge of giving the tattoos. The pain of that experience wafts to the front of my mind, and I cringe while looking down at the bright red numbers on my arm. Each of the twenty-one guys in my group are made to stand in front of one concrete chained prisoner. Before I can figure out what's about to happen, I feel my ankle become lighter as the chain is skillfully broken off by the guy chained to the concrete fence. The other chain brakes and I am free of metal restraints for the first time in days.

My heart begins to beat out of my chest, and my eyes widen as one of the prisoners start to run. It is the guy who challenged the tiny man back on the bus. I see an official point his silver gun. My whole body jumps as the blast of the weapon causes the runner to drop on the ground like a sack of potatoes. They push us all forward like nothing at all happened. But something did happen. That man is dead without a second thought from his killers. What if he was innocent like me? What if he has a family he was running to get back to? The sheer enormity of injustice that just took place fills me with so much anger I may explode into a thousand pieces. As soon as we turn the corner of the concrete fence, all of that anger is sucked out of me and what is left is the kind of fear that makes your whole body break into a cold sweat.

One-hundred feet away is a massive concrete wall that stretches out on both sides as far as my eyes can track. It rises out of the ground like it was planted there. My face turns straight toward the sky as I see how far the wall reaches up. Jay looks at me with a sad and quiet acceptance in his eyes. Our disjointed line begins to melt into the giant group of prisoners standing at the base of the wall. Almost every neck is craned upwards. Can it only have been a week ago since I was sitting at my office desk? Now I am here about to enter a seething pit of crime with no rules to moderate it.

A rectangular metal door begins to slowly creak open where the wall meets the ground. It looks strong enough to withstand an atomic bomb. The men, and some women, all begin to speak at once in scared chattering voices. Everyone was still in the clothes they were arrested in, and I can almost imagine that I am on a crowded city street corner waiting for the holographic walking light to project. After a few minutes of waiting, wailing, and waning, the door finally screeches to a halt. I stand on my toes for a better view of what lies beyond the concrete, but what I see confuses me. Even though the door is open, all I can see is a metal chamber with walls stretching as high as the concrete wall. Officials begin to yell and push us toward the chamber. I am caught up in the crowd as we all shuffle as one body. I can't turn around, but I hear multiple gunshots all around the group with screams of horror and agony following them. I guess more people tried to run.

As my feet cross the threshold of the wall, I notice that the concrete slabs that make up the barrier are about four feet thick. Once every prisoner, who didn't try and run is inside the chamber, the rectangular door begins to close behind us. I realize we are all in a sort of antechamber that keeps whoever is inside the wall from getting out. Every face is painted with terror. People begin to scramble all around, and since we are all so packed in here "scrambling" means stepping on toes. I'm in the middle of the pack, but I can see people on the borders jumping up trying to climb their way out. I lost Jay in the chaos, but a strange feeling of calm washes over me. I know that whatever awaits me next, God will either take care of me or bring me to heaven. Most likely, I will be going to heaven because about ninety percent of these people look like they eat guys like me for breakfast.

The door behind me is almost all the way closed now, and as I lose sight of the last official, a bang shakes the entire chamber, signaling the beginning of our lives behind the wall.

9. Cactus Juice

A woman with crazy eyes is weaving through the crowd and stops right in front of me. Her matted gray hair and tattered clothes show that she has been in jail much longer than I have. Her face is inches from mine, and her hot rank breath reaches my ear, "We are all doomed," she whispers then pulls back and laughs like a maniac. As if that wasn't scary enough, her eyes roll back into her head, and she faints. A small circle of people forms around her trying their best not to crush her.

A mechanical rattle jerks my focus away from the woman lying on the ground. The back wall of the chamber begins sliding open to reveal a worn dirt road with brittle grass and dark green bushes scattered on flat land. No one moves from the chamber. Suddenly, I hear another rattle and the door begins to close. All at once at least two-hundred people rush forward. I am practically being carried by the mob's mad dash. I don't get a chance to see what happened to the woman lying on the ground, but I doubt she survived the stampede of "cattle."

Once I was on the dirt road away from the confines of the chamber, I felt strangely naked. It was as if I had gotten used to being in confined spaces. Out here on this open dirt road with nothing taller than a bush, I didn't know what to do next. The mob is breaking off into factions. Some are headed down the trail, some are walking along the towering wall, and some are frozen in place. I notice Jay standing gloomily at the edge of the dirt road. I jog over to him, "Jay, which way should we go? If we head down this road, it may lead to a city."
Jay shuffles his feet, "I don't think the direction we go matters much son. Either way will lead to death."

Being freed of chains and back in the fresh air, I was starting to feel more optimistic, but Jay's morose outlook dampened my spirits, and again I feel a weight fall on my shoulders. With Jay in this state, I'm not sure if he'll be much help in whatever lies ahead of us. I finally coax him to start walking, and we head down the road into the unknown.

We've been walking for at least three hours without seeing anything but the dry brush on the side of the dirt road. Jay hasn't said much since we left the wall's border and I don't think he has even lifted his eyes from the ground. Sighing, I say, "The sun is beginning to set. Maybe we should figure out a camp for tonight?" Jay gloomily nods in response, and I begin to scan our desert-like surroundings. My eyes settle on a rock overhang about a mile off the path. "That looks like a great place to stay. At least for tonight. Maybe we can figure out some kind of food." My stomach growls at me as I remember our last form of nutrition was the frozen package of goop on the bullet tram. I feel the hollowness of hunger and my mouth is as dry as the dirt we are walking on; if we don't get food and hydration soon, Jay's prediction of death will come true.

"Justin, I don't think I can walk anymore. You go on ahead and let me rest in peace. Just let me give up."

His hopelessness reminds me of when I was

desperate enough to kill myself. If it weren't for Pastor Barrios' encouragement, I would be six feet underground. Right then, I am determined to keep Jay from giving up no matter what it takes. Jay's dry mouth speaks again, "This sucks." I shake my head and suddenly start to laugh. Jay looks at me like I've gone insane and maybe I have. Then he starts to laugh too. Nothing about our predicament is funny, but with two out of place words, Jay surmised this whole situation; this does indeed suck.

Out of breath from laughing, I puff out, "Come on Jay, let's keep going. We are almost to that overhang and who knows, maybe there's a big milkshake waiting for us." Jay starts to laugh again, and I feel his disparaging mood begin to change to a positive one.

When we reach the rock overhang, I see the remnants of weeks old trash. I guess at some point someone decided to stay here too. Out of the corner of my eye, I see Jay picking up the trash littered around. "What are you doing? I don't think we can use any of this stuff," I say while kicking an old soda can away from my foot.

"Haven't you read any survival books? Anything

can be useful. Let's gather as much as we can before it gets too dark. Then in the morning we'll spread everything out and see what we might can use." I shrug in agreement and start to pick up what I only see as garbage. Jay and I pile up our collection in a nook of the rock overhang.

I lie down on the pebbly earth with my back touching the old gray rock. My eyes gaze up to the silvery sky, and it seems as if a black canvas was dusted in glitter. Millions and millions of stars seemed to surround me like a beautiful blanket. I have never been able to see this many stars with the light pollution of cities destroying these beacons of light. I soon fall asleep under God's amazing artwork.

The next morning, I slowly stand and stretch my body. It's stiff and tired from a night of sleeping on the ground. I yawn while noticing Jay has disappeared. My eyes sweep across the endless sea of land. Jay's voice comes from behind me causing me to jump in surprise. "Justin! Guess what I found?" In each hand, he held prickly green pouches that seemed to be filled with a kind of liquid. "Here," Jay said handing me one of the pouches, "this is a cactus. I removed all the needles and pressed as much juice as I

could from the plant so we can get hydrated."

I place the greenery to my mouth. I swallow the bitter and warm liquid, feeling it seep into my stomach. Once the first bitter taste was over, I couldn't stop myself from drinking every last drop. I hadn't realized how thirsty I was. Jay smiles at me, and I notice he now has a scruffy beard with drops of cactus juice suspended on his chin.

"Now that it's light, we can see what we collected last night." I nod in agreement and begin walking toward the overhang nook where we put all the trash last night. Eventually, we have everything laid out on the blue pebble ground. There is a bunch of crumpled paper, one plastic water bottle, a ratted and hole riddled red t-shirt, three candy bar wrappers, and a cigarette lighter. I start to think about how we could use any of this. I say, "Well, I know the lighter will be helpful for starting a fire and the shirt could be used as sun cover for one of us or maybe we could tie

it into a makeshift bag?"

"I like that bag idea, and the water bottle can hold

cactus water if we hurry and collect it before the sun dries out all the plant's juice." He pauses to think about the other items, "We could use all the paper and plastic as fuel for the fire since there isn't a lot of wood out here."

"That sounds like a plan, but now we have to decide if we want to stay here another night or move on today." I hear Jay's stomach protest in hunger as if answering the question for us. We both laugh and Jay says, "I think our stomachs would appreciate us moving on and finding some food." I follow Jay to the cactus plant and am surprised to see that it looks almost human like. Two arms seem to reach for the sky in praise; I've never seen any plant like it. Jay shows me how to collect the cactus water and after getting stabbed about a hundred times by the tiny prickles, we filled the plastic bottle. Looking at the sun, I'd say it is about 08:00 and the air is already sweltering in heat. Eventually, we find our way back to the dirt road that lead us away from the wall yesterday.

Sweat rolls down my neck into my grubby blue work shirt. My gray cargo pants are suffocating, but at least they are protecting my legs from the punishment of the blazing sun rays. Jay looks even worse than I feel, poor guy. I am just glad he is in a better mood than yesterday. We stop to drink about every hour, and when our one water bottle gets low, we find another cactus. They say drinking something is supposed to help with hunger, but I don't believe that at all. I feel my stomach caving in almost as if it were trying to eat my spine. Every time I breathe my brain screams in agony. My feet feel as if a hammer had hit them over and over again and to add to my misery, the sun has burned me so badly I feel like I'm on fire. That evil ball of smoldering heat finally begins to sink down as we trudge up a rocky hill. When we reach the top, Jay stops so quickly I run into his back. "Why did we stop? Shouldn't we find shelter before..." I forget the rest of my sentence as I see the reason Jay stopped in his tracks.

10. Decisions

Down below us is a secluded shimmering city surrounded by desert. At first glance, it seems like a mirage, a cruel trick of the heat. Jay speaks in a strained whisper, almost as if he were scared to speak, lest the buildings hear him and retreat. "I guess we will camp up here for the night and head down there in the morning?" I nodded, still amazed we had a real city in front of us after only seeing sand and brittle grass for so many miles. I began making a fire by dumping the paper, candy wrappers, and wood on the hot earth and flipping on the lighter. The dry contents almost spontaneously become a blaze and my already burned face shies away from the heat. I quickly rush backward. It was almost as if the sun had sent a piece of itself to us.

We collect more cactus juice and try roasting some of the plucked green plants. Jay and I eat the cactus meat as best as we can. My stomach is grateful for the offering, but my teeth are tiring from the chewiness of our "meal." I lie on the side of my body that allows me a clear view of the dark buildings. I don't want to sleep. I don't want to take my eyes off the city just in case it is in my imagination. "Jay, are you awake?" He answers me from across our small fire with a grunt. "What do you think is down there? Better yet, who do you think is down there?"

I hear Jay shift to look at the shadowed maze of streets and skyscrapers, slightly lit by the stars and moon. "Well, I'm assuming people who would get a kick out of beating us to death. I'll tell you something son; this wall is not the way our society should've handled crime. We should've started instilling strong family values in our communities a long time ago. That way everybody would feel cared for, but instead our government, the media, gullible citizens started dividing people up into categories. Made people feel threatened. Through the year's people have turned to crime to deal with their differences," he scoffs as he pronounces his disapproval of the country's way of handling crime.

I don't say anything for a while as Jay's solution rolls around in my mind, and the more I think about it, the more I think he's right. I know that when I was traveling all alone, without a support system, I ended up wanting to die. I guess for some people being alone makes them angry, but if communities integrated family values and became one giant support system, no one would have to be alone. I wish our country's collective would've thought of that before the country divided itself into a thousand pieces.

After a while, I hear Jay snoring. My body is screaming for sleep, but my mind turns like an old recording that the listener forgot to turn off. I keep thinking about when I was a kid; imagining the endless possibilities I'd have once I got out of my town. Little did I know the "endless possibilities" would have me sitting at an office desk most of the time, then going to an empty apartment with only a few plants for comfort. I also never once imagined becoming a criminal struggling to survive. A sigh escapes my mouth like I'm trying to release all the negative feelings from my anxious mind. I soon drift off into that in-between sleep that doesn't really help my aching body.

The next morning is crisp and cool with dew lightly covering everything. I stretch my sore and stiff limbs feeling like a creaking tree. Jay is off about one-hundred yards working on collecting cactus for breakfast. I can literally feel my stomach's disappointment. We set off at a slow pace toward the city. I don't know whether to feel excited or scared so I just decide to have mixed feelings. We enter from an abandoned highway littered with three or four cars that were left behind by someone in haste to follow the government's order to leave their southern California home. Each vehicle was stripped down to a shell. The hoods were open, engines gone, windows gone, tires slashed. My mixed feelings changed to just one; fear.

As we walk further into the city, I look at the buildings once inhabited by so many souls. I still cannot believe the government convinced all these people just to get up and leave. What deal did they get promised? I shake my head to clear my thoughts. Jay walks beside me stride for stride. "Jay, what is our plan? We don't have any weapons to defend ourselves, plus, we have no idea what is in front of us right now. I mean we could be ambushed, killed, beaten," my voice starts to shake, showing the crushing fear overtaking me. I hate it.

"Look son," Jay says with as much sympathy and concern as any father could express, "I have no clue what awaits us today, tomorrow, or however much longer we each have on this Earth. I know that is terrifying for a youngster who is supposed to have fifty more years to look forward to, but the only way I can tell you to get through this is to believe that you are here in this prison world for a reason. You have to believe that no matter what Justin." He stops and grabs my wrist when he says the last sentence. His intensity takes me aback. Jay is a man of few words, but when he does speak, what he says matters.

A buffering wind tousles my hair and carries with it a horrible sound of pain. Eerie screams pierce through the maze of buildings right to where Jay and I are standing. Jay narrows his eyes in suspicion, "Let's keep going."

"Wait a minute," I say to his turned back, "What if someone needs our help. We could save someone's life today. Maybe that's is one reason we are here." I don't know what's come over me all of a sudden. I know that I am being stupid. Of course we should avoid anything or anyone associated with pain, but I just can't shake the overwhelming feeling that we should help.

"Justin, this isn't a game son. We could die or get really hurt." I know he's right so why do I still want to go toward the screams of pain that are now steadily drifting towards us?

"Please, Jay. I don't think I can live knowing we might could have saved a life but decided to run away instead." Jay sighs and hesitantly nods in a halfhearted understanding and says, "Heck, what do we have to lose?" We start walking toward the screams.

11. Losing and Finding

As we get closer, the pained sounds grow louder. I realize it isn't the sound of one man screaming; it's the sound of many. As we round the shadowed corner of a skyscraper, a muddled and bloody sight reaches my eyes. Five men were savagely fighting. Blood seeped onto the cracked sidewalk, and their grunts and shouts exploded from their bodies each time a fist hit flesh. My eyes squint up in disbelief as I see that three of these men are in some gray uniform while the other two are in tattered rags. I noticed all of this within a few seconds. Jay and I look at each other, then run into the chaos to try and save these men from the blind rage that has possessed them. I begin struggling to pull back one of the uniformed men. He shakes me off like I was merely a mosquito buzzing in his ear and jumps back into the fray. Jay is in the thick of the fight, and I see his nose bleeding and his jaw set in determination as he holds both arms out in an effort to put a barrier between the men. I start toward the guy I first tried to pull back, but a glinting flash stops me.

One of the men in tattered clothes has a shard of metal. I scream, "Jay, watch out!" but it's too late, Jay doesn't see the weapon in time. Everything around me seems to be in slow motion. Jay falls to his side as the shard of metal is ripped from his rib cage. The two rogues take the break in fighting to run the other way as I run to Jay's side. My feet seem to take years to bring me to where he is lying in a pool of blood. The three uniformed men, bruised and bleeding, look down at Jay with unsurprised expressions painted on their faces.

Everything is silent except Jay's labored breathing. Even though I haven't known him that long, hardships speed up friendships. I feel one tear move down my sunburnt cheek as I look at Jay's face twisted in pain. He turns his head to look at me one last time and says between breaths, "Justin, you're here for a reason. Don't forget that." In one final shudder, my only friend in the world dies.

One of the uniformed men cuts into my sorrow, "Your friend died honorably and we thank you." He had an accent that attached a ring to the end of each word he spoke. "We live in a gated community not too far from here that is safe and civilized. If you come with us, our leader will meet with you and decide if you get to live inside our gates. I don't think there is a reason he wouldn't let you stay, especially since you jumped in to help us." I look at the uniformed men and then back down at Jay.

"I can't leave Jay to be torn apart by animals or something." One of the other men speaks up, "We can take your friend with us in the truck. Our community has an empty lot we've been using as a graveyard." I nod my head once and the guy that first spoke nods to his buddies, and they begin to lift Jay like they are pallbearers at his funeral. I suppose they kind of are.

We walk a few blocks in silence until we come to their solar powered truck, "Hey I forgot to ask your name," one guy says while lifting Jay's lifeless body into the truck bed.

"My name is Justin Price," I say softly; still in shock from losing Jay. As soon as I said my name, all three guys look at each other with surprise and uncertainty. I have no idea why.

"Ahem," the guy that seems to be the leader clears his throat, "My name's Reed, those two are Corwin and Ben," he points to the other two guys. Reed is a tall man with dark hair and a slender nose. Corwin has darker skin and Ben's age is shown through his gray beard and peppered hair. Now that all the formalities were out of the way, Reed gets in the driver's seat and Corwin guides me to the shotgun seat while he and Ben sit in the back. After a few minutes of driving, Reed asks, "How long have you been behind the wall?"

"Just a few days, but it feels like years. Jay and I," my voice cracks thinking about my friend, I swallow, "we just arrived here in the city this morning." Reed keeps his eyes on the road but I can tell he feels bad about what happened.

He changes the subject, "Since you don't know

about the city, how about we tell you some info while we drive." I nod in agreement thinking that if their leader doesn't let me stay in their community, I'll need to know as much as I can about this place. "So to start off, I'll tell you a bit about this city. It was built a couple of years ago and they named it Oasis since it's in the middle of a desert. Judging by your sunburn, I am sure you've figured that out. Anyhow, our community sends out us three to pick up supplies, meds, and whatever else we can find in the city. We're called collectors. There are also guards and brains. Guards do just as the name implies by protecting the community and also making sure everybody stays in line. Brains make all the big decisions like when to send out collectors and what supplies we need the most. The system is simple but it works well."

I am amazed that they've created an entire tiny civilization in this god-forsaken prison. When I was just a regular citizen, the government made it sound like behind the wall was filled with primitive and animalistic savages. I guess they don't know everything. "How'd you guys start your, uh, community?"

"I think Corwin can explain that the best," Reed

says passing the responsibility of conversation to Corwin.

"Well, Justin, I was in one of the first groups to be sent behind the wall and a bunch of us formed a team of sorts. We walked for an eternity but we eventually found Oasis. For a while, all of us holed up in a skyscraper, but eventually we found a few cars that worked for us and had the idea to move into a gated community just a few miles outside of the city." He makes it sound like they've settled in nicely and if he was one of the first waves to come here that must mean he's been here a while.

The truck jumps after hitting a pothole and we are soon out of the tall building's shadows and into the hot sun of the desert. Soon the dust turns into tall green grass and bushes. I hear a thump in the truck bed and an image of Jay getting tossed around in the back crosses my mind making me cringe.

Eventually, I drift off but I wake up at the sound of Ben and Corwin quietly talking about something. I keep pretending to be asleep and try to pick up their conversation, "It's just a coincidence. Do you know how many people could have the last name Price?" My ears immediately prick up at the mention of my last name.

"I see your point Ben, but they look just alike. Genetics don't lie man. If this kid actually is related to him how do you think Trick is going to take the news?" Huh? If I'm related to who? What are they talking about?

I hear Ben's voice reply, "I doubt Trick would take too kindly to some kid kicking him out of being next in line after all the work he's put into getting the community in shape." They stop taking, but I wish I could've found out more.

I feel Reed shake my shoulder in an effort to wake me, "We're here!"

I open my eyes still really confused about what I just heard. An ornate and large gate stands in front of the truck and two men standing guard push it open for us to enter. As we pass by, I take notice that they're holding assault rifles. Ben sticks his head in the front, "Hey Reed, let's go ahead and take the kid straight to the hut," he directs his head toward me now, "The Hut's this huge mansion where the leader lives and all the brains work." Ben falls back to his seat and I quietly take in the neighborhood. I have no doubt that very rich people used to live here because every house must have cost millions of dollars to build. Even the sidewalks seemed to be paved in silver. After a few minutes of driving through, I realize this is a bigger compound than I thought. There are at least fifty houses within the towering black gates that used to protect rich people from criminals.

Reed must have noticed my surprise because he says, "Yeah, the size of the place is a bit overwhelming at first but it's really easy to learn where everything is. See the houses on the outskirts are smaller and less grand and as you get further into the middle, the bigger the houses get." We pull up to the biggest house I've ever seen. It has double staircases that lead up to a huge porch that shelters the doubled front door. I bet the height is at least eight of me, and I'm five-nine.

I take my cues from the three guys and get out of the car. Ben says, "Justin, Reed is going to take you inside and Corwin and I will make sure your friend is properly buried. We really can't thank you enough for helping us fight off those rogues." Corwin is already in the driver's seat and they soon use the circle drive to head back down the street. "You ready to go in?" He doesn't wait for an answer before he begins walking up the stairs, so I just follow. Ben and Corwin's conversation is still tugging the back of my mind.

"Just wait right here. I'll go and talk to him first." Reed enters the leader's lair through oak doors that seem to have been grown right from the floor. This entire hallway is littered in art and burnt orange paint. I feel like I'm in some weird alternate universe and soon I'll be transported back to my easy life in Baltimore. Every situation that has brought me here has been as bizarre as the former; getting arrested, meeting Jay, surviving in the desert, losing Jay, and now this. Nothing that happens next can be as insane as what I've been through, right?

Reed comes back to the hallway with the same strange look on his face that he, Corwin, and Ben had when I told them my name. "You can go on in Justin." I take a deep breath and push open the heavy oak door. I find myself standing in a large study with a huge window straight across from the door and bookshelves lining the walls on both sides. In the center of the window is a very large desk with a very large man sitting behind it. That man looks exactly like my father.

12. Catching Up

I stare at him frozen in time. I can't find air to breathe. Why is he here? Is it even him? My mind is racing with thousands of questions, but I can't think of one to ask.

"Justin? Is it really you?" the large man stands up, his voice quavering with the threat of tears. He begins to walk closer and I can now tell that this man really is my father. His brown hair is grayer now and his eyes seem laden with dark memories. Now the conversation between Ben and Corwin makes more sense. I can see my father still seems to put a lot of effort into creating a smile, but he makes up for his lacking facial expressions with a hug. I didn't realize how much I've missed him over the years.

"Dad, I can't believe you're here right in front of

me. What happened?" the man I knew growing up would never do anything bad enough to get here. Maybe he was imprisoned for self-defense like me.

His face twists into sadness, "We'd better take a seat." We both sit on a couch in the corner of the study, "I wish you could have found out a different way, but your mother is dead. Sorry to say it so bluntly but I find it isn't good to beat around the bush." My heart sinks to my stomach, "Your mom went to the kitchen for some water really late one night and a robber had gotten in without us knowing. The next thing I hear is your mother scream; then a gun goes off. By the time officials got to our house, it was too late. She was gone."

I am quiet for a minute, trying to process this, "But why did you get arrested?" I asked numbly with overwhelming grief after losing Jay and my mother all in one day.

"When the officials pulled up they saw the blood on my hands from holding your mother and they automatically assumed that I had killed her. Two days later, I was on some bullet tram to California." He looks at his hands as if remembering the color of Mom's blood.

"I'm sorry I wasn't there for you guys. If I would've been there maybe…"

"Stop right there Justin. There is nothing either of us could have done. You can't blame yourself when bad things happen. Just put it behind you and look forward. And since I truly believe that, I won't ask you how you got here. However, I do have to know what crime you committed." Seeing the question of why on my face he clarifies, "You see, I set a rule for this community that the only people who can live within the safety of our gates are the ones who have been *falsely* imprisoned for one reason or another. You'd be surprised at how many there are."

The fact that my own dad would throw me out if I didn't meet a certain standard proves that he is definitely not the same man that raised me and I can't tell if that's good or bad. Thinking back to what got me here, the image of my kidnapper's cold dead stare pops in my head. I tell my dad the truth, "I was arrested for self-defense."

Dad smiles in relief and his broad shoulders seem to relax, "Welcome to the community son. You'll stay with me of course! Follow me and I'll show you a room you can have." As we walk through the house, I am

81

amazed at how many hallways there are. I hope I can find my way out again. Dad stops to open one of the hundreds of doors. I follow him in and see a four post king-sized bed on the back wall with two large windows bookending it. On the left wall is a fireplace big enough to climb in. "Wow," I breathe out, "This room is amazing; especially after the places I've been sleeping."

Dad chuckles and I take into account that he seems so much more relaxed than I remember him, "I'm glad you like it. I just can't believe you right here in front of me. I never imagined I'd see you again. I honestly wish you weren't here, but I sure am glad you are." He laughs again, "I guess that didn't make much sense but you know what I mean. Now tomorrow, I'll have Corwin give you a full tour of the community and you can decide if you want to work with another department with me." I don't really know what he means by other departments, but right now I just want to jump in that bed and sleep. As soon as my dad closes the room's door, that's exactly what I do.

13. The Community

I wake up to someone knocking on the door. For half a second, I have no clue where I am but then yesterday's events flood my memory, and suddenly I feel tired again. "Hey kid, it's me, Corwin. I'm supposed to show you around today, and that means that you can't keep sleeping like a bear in the winter." I groan and roll out of bed onto my feet. I still can't believe I got to sleep in an actual bed.

I don't have any clothes to change into; I just slept in the same clothes I've been wearing. There's a mirror on the wall beside the door, and when I move in front of it, I almost shout. My hair has grown into a shaggy bird's nest, and I have a beard. My work shirt looks more brown than blue from the desert's dust, and my beat up black and white sneakers have holes in the bottom of them. Corwin knocks again, and when I open the door, the first thing I do is ask for a razor.

Corwin just laughs and takes me to a bathroom down the hall that is probably the size of my apartment back in Baltimore. He gets me a razor and clean clothes says, "Alrighty then, I'll give you ten minutes. If you're not ready by then, I'm going on without you." I nod and close the red wooden door. I flip the light switch on, silently thanking the inventor of solar powered roofing tiles. I go over to the large walk-in shower and turn the dial. Water pours down, quickly creating a beautiful puddle on the tile ground. I laugh, not able to believe how lucky I am to be here.

I quickly peel off my dirty and worn clothes and step into the steamy air of the shower. The warm water falls on my back washing away every particle of the last nine days. The white tile of the shower floor looks brown until the dirty water is washed down the silver drain. I jump out of the shower, shave, throw on the new clothes that end up being a little baggy, and quickly open the door to see Corwin waiting with his arms crossed. I take note

84

that he is now in regular clothes and not in his gray uniform from yesterday, probably because it was all bloody and torn. "Let's go," he starts walking. I follow him feeling like an entirely new person.

We walk a short way to an empty lot with brown grass surrounding dirt mounds that I'm assuming are graves. Corwin confirms my guess, "I thought the graveyard would be a good place to start the tour. This was just an empty lot that no one had built on yet. Sadly, we needed a graveyard right when we first got here because of some sickness that hit. Your friend is the first one to be buried here that didn't die from a sickness," he coughed as if trying to soften his words, "I'll show you where your friend is buried. Then, when you're ready, we can head on to the Artillery House." We reach the freshly placed pile of dirt, and he steps a few feet away to give me some privacy. I look around, and there must be at least ten mounds of dirt just like Jay's. Each one has a wooden cross with a name on it. There's also a stone in the very back of the lot with some crude handwriting scratched on. I look at it closely, and it reads…

85

Here Lie the Dead
May They Rest in Peace

Corwin must have noticed my gaze because he says, "That stone's kind of like a symbolic headstone for all of the graves. You see, most people thought the crosses were better markers, but some thought stone was better, so we just sort of compromised." I look back down at Jay's unmarked pile of dirt. "We will get a cross for your friend made too. We just didn't know his last name." I stare at the ground that covers my friend. In remorse, I realize that I don't

know his last name either.

"His first name is 'Jay' and I would like his last name to say Price. He was more like my family than anything else." I feel my eyes threatening to spill tears, so I tell Corwin, "Let's get on with the tour. I'm sure there's a lot you have to show me."

We walked past the bigger houses and moved to the outskirts of the community. I didn't see one person. "How many people do you guys have living here?"

"Last I heard, we are seventy-six strong; including

you. Sometime in the next few months, we will be seventy-seven."

"Oh really? Why's that?" I ask, confused again. I can't wait till I learn how this place works.

"You remember Ben from yesterday, yeah?" I nod yes, "Well, he and his sweetheart Milly are expecting the stork to drop by soon. She was a part of the first group, along with me. Ben came to the community later on, and they just hit it off." He laughs good-heartedly at the memory, "We even held them a little wedding ceremony a while back. Not one of us is a preacher, but it's the thought that counts, right?"

I smile and think about how this isn't as savage a life as I was expecting when the officials threw me inside the wall. The sun is shining, the sky is blue, and for the first time in a while, I feel safe. We soon come to a brick house that is smaller than my dad's but still pretty large by any standard. "This, my friend, is our artillery. Every kind of weapon that we've found over the years is in this house. Before we go in, I have to tell you not to touch anything. The community guards run this house, and sometimes I think they like to guard their inventory more than the gate."

"Okay, no problem," as we walk through the door I am greeted by a stony-faced gentleman sitting in a dining chair right in front of the door. He only gives Corwin a slight nod to say hello. I notice he has a gun strapped to his right side. We quickly pass him by and enter the first room. With its light gray walls and a closet to the side, it must have been a guest room when people actually lived here. Now, it is filled with knives, hammers, and a bunch of other intimidating tools. "Well, here is the manual room. Every weapon here would have to used by hand. Knives are hung up on this back wall, shards of sharp metal in the closet, and random stuff over here," Corwin points to some built in shelves to the left of us. "Upstairs is where the good stuff is," he gives me a wink and we start to climb the stairs. The first room we enter isn't as full as the one downstairs, but there are enough guns in there to make me not want to step out of line. In some ways, it reminds me of my old job's defense room with all their weapons, even though this is on a much smaller scale.

"I guess you must've noticed we don't have as many guns as we have manual weapons, but we have enough to protect us. I won't show you the other rooms just because they're sort of boring. One's filled with ammunition and one is where the General lives," Corwin pauses and when I don't say anything, he starts walking out of the gun room and back downstairs, "The General is the guy in charge of the guards. He is a hardcore army guy, but no one knows how he got here, except for your dad I guess. Do you think you'll decide to be a guard?"

"Honestly, I have no idea. What are the choices again?" Corwin laughs at my lack of knowledge as we walk out of the house and he invites me to sit on the porch chairs.

"Alright, so you have the options of guard, brain, farmer, or collector, which is what Ben, Reed and I do for the community. We're the only three right now, but it is a pretty dangerous job. Heck, you saw that for yourself yesterday. All we were trying to do was gather up some medical supplies for Doc and those rogues came outta nowhere with fists swinging."

Was that seriously only yesterday? It feels like

weeks have gone by since I saw Jay die. "Why didn't you three bring guns with you?"

"Good question kid. See we usually do bring guns with us, but since we only needed to run into the city for a couple of things, Reed, who's in charge of the collectors, meaning Ben and me, he decided we didn't need them. It was a bad call that would've killed us if you and Jay hadn't shown up." I sigh, if only Reed would've decided to bring guns. Jay wouldn't be dead. But maybe this all happened for a reason. I mean it got me here to my dad, right? I guess I just have to trust that God has a plan and this heartache of losing my friend is part of it.

I look at Corwin's dark skin and the sympathy in his eyes. I decide that I need to get some things straight about this community so I say "I have so many questions right now. Do you mind if I just ask them all at once?" Corwin smiles and shrugs. I take that as a yes. "First off what does each job do exactly? Whose Doc and can we find some food soon? I'm
starving." We both laugh at that last question.

"To answer you first question, guards are the muscle in our community. About thirty-two people chose that job. Twelve of them are women and let me just tell you they scare me, and I am on their side! If some rogues try to break into the gate or, heaven forbid, get past the gate, the guards would make sure it's the last thing they do. The next department has guys like your father. We call them brains because mainly all they do is think about everybody's needs and such. Basically, they're our little community's government; however, we do *not* call them that because the sick, evil, stupid government outside the wall put every person in our community here for the wrong reasons. We avoid the using the 'g' word at all cost."

He told me about not using the term 'government' so fiercely it made me wonder what made him so angry. Why'd they put him behind the wall? "Sorry for the ranting, but I just get so torn up about it. They took me away from my family for no reason at all." I saw his eyes glistening with tears under the shade of the porch, but in one blink those tears were gone, "Anyway, including your dad, seven guys are brains. Speaking of your dad, he will be introducing you to everybody at a meeting tonight." I open my mouth to ask what that meeting will be like but he stops me, "Your dad can tell you more about that after we finish the tour. We can go to the farm after we eat. It's a little bit of a drive, but we got all day. Now, the farm is one other job you could do. We have about thirty farmers right now, and they just take care of our plants and animals. The last job is what I am, a collector. You already know what we do. As soon as one "department" needs some supplies Reed gathers Ben and I up and we go on a little scavenger hunt." He pauses to take a breath after all that talking. "That's a lot of information so let's go find some grub while you absorb all of it."

I am still wondering about Doc, but I assume that he's the community doctor since Corwin said they were out looking for medical supplies for him. Maybe I'll get to meet him on the tour. Right now I am just excited about getting actual food and not cactus.

"This house is our community Nutrients House. We keep all of our farmed food here, as well as anything we can find back in the city," Corwin tells me. It's a quirky house with its green door and yellow siding. The unusual colors remind me of the orange paint my dad has on his walls. The inside of the house is even more peculiar. Whoever lived in these houses must have gotten some interesting interior design advice. Corwin led me straight to the kitchen, "In these cabinets, we have vegetables, and in the fridge, we have fresh eggs and even some milk if that cow is still on the farm. May even have some cured ham left."

"You guys keep animals too?" I said while opening up the neon-pink colored fridge and grabbing three light brown eggs and the last piece of ham. Corwin was pulling out a pan for me to use.

"Oh yeah, you'll see them after lunch. We have too many chickens to count, rabbits, goats, pigs, and one milking cow. We are hoping to get a horse, but no one really knows how to take care of one and frankly, no one knows how to ride one either, but we're all just too proud to admit that."

I ate fast, and that quieted the monster that has been clawing at my stomach for what seems like forever. After I had eaten enough to feel my belly distended in delight, we jumped in the solar powered truck that I rode in yesterday and headed to the farm. "It takes about twenty minutes to get there. Us collectors found it a while back. Most of the fields were still growing crops and the people that lived there before the government kicked them out had just set their animals loose. Most of those animals just stayed on the property just waiting for their owner to come feed them. It's sad really. That farm was probably owned by the same family for generations."

"That's very sad. I wonder where that family is now." I couldn't imagine being forced out of my home so it could be taken over by prisoners. A newscast that I heard when they first began building the wall said that many people were resisting the government's request that they leave and I don't blame them. I wonder how the government convinced them to relocate.

Pretty soon we were pulling up to a white farmhouse that was so old it didn't even look powered by solar energy. To the right, I saw a strong barn with a few chickens running around catching bugs. I followed Corwin to the back of the house and was surprised to see rows and rows of plants. In between these rows were the farmers who all look up from their work to glance at me. One man whose skin looked like tan leather and had eyes that looked like they've seen many years greets me with a firm handshake. His hand feels as if he has picked up a shovel thousands of times. "Hey there. You must be Justin. New travels fast 'round here," remarked the farmer. "My name is Fred, Freddy to my friends. I'm the head of the farming department. Gosh, you look just like your daddy. Corwin let me show you some things we need y'all to find for us," Fred talks so fast I have a hard time keeping up with what he says. Corwin doesn't tell me to follow them, so I don't. Only a small part of the field is being used now. I can tell that before the wall was built this was a huge agricultural farm that probably supplied Oasis with food.

"Okay Freddy, I'll tell Reed the list and we will plan an excursion real soon," Corwin glances at me, "Ready kid? We only have one more stop, and that's Docs. I have to drop off some of the supplies we got yesterday. Bye Freddy."

"It was good to meet you, Freddy," he gives me a look that could probably curdle their cow's milk.

"I said only my friends get to call me Freddy. You're not my friend." His hard face softens into a laugh

95

that will probably keep me up tonight. It was just downright creepy.

I find myself not wanting to talk much on the ride back, and I am glad that Corwin seems to be happy with some silence. I stare out the window, and the sun is casting a golden glow on the green land as we pass it by; it is so beautiful I forget to breathe. The green gives way to desert and memories of suffering heat come rushing back. My skin is still red and peeling from having to walk in that terrible openness. It's funny because while I was being transported to the wall, all I wanted was to be in a wide open space. The desert was a wide open space by all physical means, but the sun was like a guard that continuously beat its prisoner.

Corwin pulls the truck up to the guarded gates and then he turns to the outer edge of the neighborhood where the smaller houses reside. He stops in front of a quaint white house that has a wood carved sign welcoming its visitors. On closer inspection, it says Doc's Place. I guess I will get to meet Doc after all.

14. The Girl

When we enter Docs, I can see that the downstairs of the house has been completely stocked with medical supplies. Bottles of pills line the shelves of a built-in cabinet next to an electric fireplace. A bulky examination chair has taken over what once looked to be the living room; I bet that was fun to carry in here. The stairs that stare at you when walking in must lead up to where Doc lives. Kind of like how the General lived upstairs at the Artillery House.

Everything in here is white; the walls, the ceiling, even the doorknobs. The only thing different was the rich hardwood floors. It looked, and felt, clean. We move to the living room as Corwin calls out, "Hey Doc, I've got your supplies you asked for waiting out in the truck." My ears pick up footsteps, and I turn around to find the most beautiful girl I've ever seen descending the staircase.

"Hi, Corwin. Dad is in one of the back rooms with Milly, but I can help get the supplies in," the beautiful girl has a voice like a bird's song. Her honey colored hair shines like gold as she passes the light peeking through the window shades. She notices me for the first time and seems a bit surprised, but in a moment her eyes clear with understanding, "You must be the new guy. Justin, is it?" I nod, suddenly unable to move my tongue. She reaches out to shake my hand. Her soft skin on mine makes every nerve in my arm tingle with electricity. "My name is Annabelle, but please call me Anne. I'm Doc's daughter."

Corwin glances back and forth between the two of us with a knowing and meddling smile, "Well, maybe I should give you both some time to get to know each other. I'll pull the truck around back and say hey to Doc and Milly." He walks out of the living room down a narrow hallway, and I really wish he hadn't left me here. I still don't think my tongue will work.

Anne looks at me and rolls her eyes good-heartedly, obviously catching on to Corwin's game of

Cupid. "You want to sit in the kitchen? I'll get us some waters." I smile and follow her to the stark white kitchen on the other side of the stairs. We take a seat at their breakfast table which oddly enough was a robin egg blue color. She sets two glasses on the table and takes a seat.

ANNE'S PERSPECTIVE

When Dad told me the leader's son was found I thought he'd be some middle-aged creep; I never imagined him being so handsome. With his deep brown eyes that seem to encompass me in warmth, his strong jawline, and gentle ambiance has my stomach filled with butterflies. He hasn't said one word since he got here. Maybe if I ask him a question, it'll encourage him. I take a sip of water and ask, "So what'd you get thrown behind the wall for?"

He looks sad for a moment, and I worry I said something I shouldn't have, but he answers me anyway "I was out on a drive for my job and these three escapees captured me. I had to, um," he glances at me then back down to his fingers that were tracing lines into the condensation of his water glass, "I had to kill one of them. The officials claimed it was a murder, so here I am."

"I'm so sorry. That's sounds horrible." Now I look down at my glass feeling a bit awkward.

Justin smiles sympathetically, putting me at ease, "Don't be sorry, someone once told me that I was here for a reason and I believe him." He seems to be caught in a memory for a moment, and then his whole mood seems to shift as he turns the conversation's focus toward me. "So how'd you get to be here? You don't have to answer if you don't want too. I just noticed you don't have an arm tattoo."

Most days I try to avoid the memories that question evokes, but I've never really felt this comfortable with someone so fast. It must mean I can trust him not to judge my dad and me.

I take a deep breath and dive into my memories that I haven't revisited in a while. "I'm sure you saw on the news how some people were resisting the government's order to leave," he nods and I keep going, "Well, my mom, dad and I were some of those people. My dad was a doctor, and my mom ran an apple orchard that had been in her family for generations. We loved everything about our home. Almost every day I'd take a walk through the rows of trees watching the drones that collected the apples. I could spend hours and hours sitting under those trees, reading books, painting, just doing nothing. Plus, we were close to the ocean. It was only about a ten-minute bike ride to the beach." I sigh wistfully remembering how enchanted my life had been.

Justin says something, pulling me from my memories, "Your eyes light up when you talk about your old home. You must've really loved it. I understand why your family didn't want to leave." I blush at his observation, and I am pretty sure I see his cheeks turn a shade of pink too.

"Wow, you're the first person that I've told who didn't say something along the lines of 'You should've gotten out when you could've.' And looking back I guess those people were right, but at the time we just figured there's no way the government would actually be crazy enough to go through with making an entire half of a state a glorified prison. Obviously, we underestimated them. Our house was very close to where they began building the wall. In fact, I could see it from my room. As soon as the low caliber criminals finished the sections of the wall that were still in our view, these officials in silver suits came to our house and tried to force us to leave. My mother shoved me into a closet and then I heard shouting and a really loud crash. I ran to the foyer and saw that my dad was knocked out and my mother was lying in a pool of her own blood. Those cowards pushed her, she hit her head and, and..." I start crying. I hate that I do, especially in front of Justin. I just can't help it. Every single time I remember what happened it's like my brain can't process it, so I have to purge out the unbearable sadness with tears.

Justin stands up and comes over to my chair. He brings himself down to my eye level and takes my hand. Of course, I am still crying but he doesn't seem the least bit embarrassed. Not even my dad acts like this when I sob. We both stand up, and he wraps me in arms, and for the first time since I saw my mom on that floor, I cried without holding back. I feel Justin's arms wrapped around me as I let go all of those bottled up emotions that explode from me like a soda can spewing everywhere after being shaken.

Eventually, I am all cried out, and I look up to his face. I'm surprised to find that he is crying too. As his hand comes to my cheek and wipes away the tears he says, "I found out yesterday that my mom is dead too. I am so sorry. I'm so so sorry." He takes a step back, letting me go only when he knew I was okay.

Our eyes meet again, and something inside of my heart knows that whatever terrible events brought us both here were meant to happen. Justin seems to sense this too until someone's voice cuts through our revelation. It's my dad and Corwin. I wipe away the rest of my tears and put on a smile.

JUSTIN'S PERSPECTIVE

As I regrettably take back my arms from holding Anne, I can't help but think that she is the strongest person on Earth to have stayed here after losing her mom that way. We catch each other's eye, now shy from our emotional confessions. As I look into her intelligent grey-blue eyes, the air crackles with attraction. Suddenly, I hear

Corwin's voice, "Hey Justin," he stops as if he could sense something had just happened between Anne and me, "I would like you to meet Doc. He's the man you'll come to with all your health complaints," he jokes, not missing a beat.

I smile at an older man with a kind smile and Anne's eyes. I do my best to give him the best handshake I have. For some reason, I want to impress this guy. I look over at Anne, and I think I know why. He says, "Nice to meet you, Justin! I was so excited to meet the leader's son. You must be about Anne's age."

"It's nice to meet you too. And I believe you're right; I'm twenty-three sir." I notice Corwin behind Doc puckering his lips at Anne and she moves over to hit the back of his head, laughing all the while.

"Yep, my wonderful daughter here just turned twenty-one last month." I hear a woman in the back asking if Anne was there. "She sure is Milly. Anne, would you mind going over some last minute questions Milly has about taking care of the baby?"

Anne starts to leave the kitchen and waves goodbye as she says, "See you at the meeting tonight

Justin." I wave back feeling a little lightheaded.

Doc seems to have caught on to the energy in the room and chuckles to himself, "I'll have to keep my eye on you."

Corwin laughs, "Doc, Justin's a blooming hero. I can personally vouch for his character," after giving Doc a slap on the back and shooting me a wink he asks, "Hey kid you ready to go back to The Hut? Your dad wanted me to drop you off at his office after the tour." I nod, and we are soon back in the truck.

"So, you got a little something for the doctor's daughter, huh?" Corwin asks mischievously.

Playing along with his bantering I say, "Aww shut up, man. I just met her. I'm only trying to figure out how to survive in this place with all of you savages running around."

Corwin laughs as he pulls the truck into The Hut's circle drive. I jump out and close the car door. "I had a good time today greenie. I'll see you tonight for the meeting. Make sure you clean up real nice for Miss Anne, ya hear?" He guns the truck, waving out the window as he goes. I head inside, trying to remember how to get to my dad's office.

After wandering around the endless hallways, I finally find the double oak doors. Dad is searching his collection of books. When I come in, he plucks one out and turns to greet me. "Justin! I've been thinking all day about how amazing it is that you found us. What do you think about our little community?"

"I think it's incredible. Everything seems so organized and," I glance up searching for the right word, "self-sufficient. I think I'm going to like it here."

"Glad to hear that son because I want to officially introduce you to the community tonight. I've called everyone for a meeting at the pool patio in a few hours." He motions for me to come to the window and I look down to see a barn-sized pavilion in the backyard, right beside a drained pool filled with dead leaves. "We usually hold the community meetings every two weeks, but this is a special occasion! We're going to have music, food, and all the works. You'll get to meet everyone and announce what job you've chosen. You have decided, yes?" He looks at me expectantly.

"Well, I haven't actually figured that out yet. There was just so much information on the tour today; nothing has really sunk in yet."

"Not to worry, you still have a few hours to think about it. Although, I do hope you end up deciding to work here with your old man. No pressure, simply pick what you feel you'd be the best at."

I smile at him suddenly exhausted as this already long day catches up to me, "I'll be thinking about it. Right now I think I'll go rest up for the meeting if that's alright."

"Of course that's alright. I left some nicer clothes on your bed that you can change into for tonight and for the future I'll put in an order to the Collectors for a few wardrobe pieces for you." I nod and leave his office.

I find my room pretty easily and walk right in. A plaid button up shirt along with khaki pants are folded neatly at the foot of the bed just like Dad said. I ignore them for now, kicking off my shoes and laying down. I promise myself I'll only rest my eyes for a few minutes.

15. The Meeting

I had this crazy dream of being chased. I awake in a panic, my breath fast as I come back to the land of the living. I realize I slept way longer than I wanted too. I groggily throw on the folded clothes and do a few jumping jacks to get my blood flowing again. I head to the bathroom to freshen up. I splash my face, brush my teeth, and do an overall check of myself thinking the whole time if I could impress Anne in this plaid shirt.

When I enter back into the hallway, I see my dad. "Oh good, you're all ready to go. I told all the Brains to meet us at the patio a bit early so you could meet them first." I follow him downstairs, suddenly feeling nervous.

The sunset is casting shadows over The Hut's

backyard as I follow my dad past the empty pool and onto the covered patio. There I see a few card tables set up with lots of vegetables and a full sized turkey that I guess came straight from the farm. At the end of the tables, four men are standing in a circle cutting up and laughing. My dad interrupts their conversation, "My friends, this is my son and our newest community member. Justin these are the Brains of our community." He begins naming them off from left to right, "That's Jorge, Fernando, Jacks, and Trick. Trick here is my right-hand man." Trick acts like he can't stand being near my dad or maybe it's me he doesn't want to be around. Corwin and Ben's conversation I overheard comes back to me. This is the guy they said might see me as a threat to his position as the next leader. He looks like he could slit my throat within two seconds, so I decide to avoid him at all cost.

Soon the rest of the community arrives. There are so many new faces, and after my dad introduces me to every one of them, he walks off to mingle with the community. I stand alone, taking in the lively scene. The food hasn't been touched yet, but a few people are standing by the table to make sure they're first in line. I've already forgotten most of these people's names, but I remember the one's I've already met; like Fred, the creepy laugh guy, who I see go over to talk with Trick about something that involves looking over at me. Reed is talking with Corwin, and Ben is coming over to give me a handshake, "Justin I'd like you to meet my lovely wife, Milly." I shake her hand as she says hello I recognize her voice from Doc's place.

"Nice to meet you, Milly. Congratulations to you both." I motion to her swollen belly.

"Thank you. We are very excited!" Milly says. They walk over to talk with some of the farmers that I've already met. I search the crowd again looking for someone very in particular. Where is she?

I see my dad standing on one of the many picnic tables at the front of the patio, "The meeting is ready to begin," he waits till everyone is quiet. "Yesterday, as I am sure most of you've heard, our brave collectors were in Oasis when ambushed by rogues. They would've surely been killed if not for our new community member Justin and his late friend Jay jumping in to help. Justin, please come join me up here." I feel my face heat up like a stove burner as I step up onto the wooden table with my dad. "I am proud to accept my son Justin Price into the community." The seventy-something audience claps. I finally see Anne's golden hair in the back of the crowd standing with Doc. She smiles as I catch her eye. My dad asks "Justin, have you decided which department you will serve the community with?"

He and everyone else looks at me expectantly,

"I... um, I've decided to work with my dad. If you'll have me of course." I say to him.

He smiles and grabs my wrist to hold up my arm like I am a heavyweight champion, "Justin Price, a Brain, my son, and our newest community member." Everyone claps and some even give whoops of approval, all except one. Trick is standing to the side with his arms crossed and a disgusted look on his face. He soon walks off like he can't be here one more second.

"Let's eat!" my dad yells making every person head toward the food tables. I hop down and head toward Anne.

ANNE'S PERSPECTIVE

He has this goofy but cute grin on his face as he walks to me, "Hey Anne, I'm glad to see you. I was starting to think you didn't get to come."

"We were a little late. My dad takes forever to get ready," Dad steps in and says "Hey don't blame me, blame my hair. It takes time to look this great." He comically runs his hand through his short gray hair, and we all laugh.

Justin eats with my dad and I. We talk about science, politics, books; deep topics that make me like him even more. Soon some of the farmers begin playing music with their old guitars. I see Milly pulling Ben out in the empty space of the patio to dance. More of the community's couples join in, and it puts a smile on my face. Justin stands up beside me holding out his hand, "Would you like to dance?"

The butterflies in my stomach come back. I smile playfully, "I'd love to, but only if you let me lead." He laughs, and we head to the floor, my hand in his.

He unsurely puts his other hand on my waist, and we begin to dance. Soon all the awkwardness melts away

112

and so does the rest of the world. I put my head on his chest and for the first time in a while I feel safe.

Eventually the song ends and the spell that make us the only people on Earth breaks. We move away from each other and applaud the band like everyone else. I look at him and blush when I see him smiling at me. To cover the redness in my face, I rush to say, "I guess I'd better get home. Thanks for the dance." I wish I could express how what just happened was so much more than a dance, but by the way his eyes shine I think he already understands. "I hope you have a good first day tomorrow. If you don't have any plans for lunch, you can join me at the Nutrient House around twelve."

Justin looks a bit nervous when I mention his first day, but then he flirtatiously says, "I'll make sure I don't have plans." I blush again and say goodbye as I rejoin my dad.

JUSTIN'S PERSPECTIVE

As she walks away, I can't help wishing she would to come back. I can still feel her hand in mine, and I realize I feel more connected to her than anyone I have ever met. She's gorgeous, smart, strong; I can't wait until it's twelve tomorrow.

16. First Few Months

My first day as a Brain. I can do this. These two sentences are what I tell myself all the way to my dad's office. I enter to find Dad and Trick are having a hushed conversation that ends when I enter the room. "Sorry to interrupt. I'll step out."

"Justin, my boy, please come in. Ole' Trick and I were just discussing something that should be water under the bridge by now." He shoots an angry glance at Trick and the tough man quickly walks out and slams the door behind him.

I wince. I hope that anger wasn't because of me. "So Dad, what will I be doing as a Brain?"

"Well, first off you'll need your own office." We arrive at a room that is a bit smaller than my bedroom, and my dad tells me what I'll be doing, "Your job is to determine what the community needs the most. You can do that by going out into the community and talking with people. If you see an area where we can become more efficient talk to the head of the department, you think needs help. Got all that?" I nod and move toward the cherry wood desk in the room, "Good deal. If you have any questions, feel free to ask me or any of the Brains. Their offices are all on this hall." My dad closes the door behind him, leaving me on my own.

I decide to go out in the community, and the first place I go is the farm. I talk with a few people then head back to my office. I analyze the farmer's opinions and suggestions for quite a while. The old grandfather clock in the room chimes twelve. I leave for lunch with excitement in my heart that I get to see Anne.

For the next few months my days are just like the first; talk to the people, think about what they say, meet Anne for lunch (and sometimes for dinner). Each day our connection grows stronger, and each day I think there's no way I can like her more than I do now, but I always

116

prove myself wrong. By the thirty-fifth day here in the community I was beginning to find a rhythm. A sense of normalcy washed over me.

I am walking back to The Hut smiling as I think of how blessed I am to have found this relatively normal life behind the Prison Wall. The sun is shining warmly, and I can see The Hut's roof peeking out from atop the hill when suddenly I feel someone grab my t-shirt. I'm yanked in between two houses whose shadows create a black air that seems to swallow the nameless force that pulled me here.

17. The Truth

My eyes adjust to the dark alley, and I see Trick looking nervously around to make sure no one saw him dragging me in here. "Trick? You'd better have a good reason for this or so help me I'll get you thrown out of this community."

"Look I'm sorry for the ambush okay, but I can't keep quiet another day. The guilt is eating me alive. I have never been able to keep a secret, especially one that is so evil." This guy is as crazy as a loon. I begin to walk out of the alley, but he pulls me back by my arm. "Justin I'm not the villain, your dad is. Please hear me out."

"What the heck is that supposed to mean?" I ask confused.

Trick sighs "I've been with your dad the entire time

since he got arrested. We were in the same prison, on the same bullet tram, and we stuck together once we got behind the wall. He has told me things he doesn't want anyone to know. He's a fraud, Justin. He's gotten everybody believing this community only allows in people that have been wronged by justice, but it's not true. The very leader of this place, your dad, deserves to be behind this wall."

"What are you talking about? The only reason my dad was arrested was because he tried to save my mom's life. When the officials found him, he was just at the wrong place at the wrong time. They both were. He didn't commit any crime. You're just lying to try and make me leave so you can be the next leader." My voice begins to rise with anger.

Trick shakes his head, "He wasn't helping your mom. He killed her."

I stare in shock. "That... that can't be true."

"I wish it weren't. See before we found Corwin and the others your dad and I were lost in the desert for days. We both thought we were going to die and I guess he had to let someone know the truth about why he got arrested. He told me every gory detail about how he killed his own wife, your mother. I was disgusted. Eventually, we found Corwin and your dad spun this whole story about how his wife was killed by some robber. Sounds like he told the exact same lie to you. When he took over the community and set this rule about how no one was allowed in the gates unless they were falsely imprisoned, I begged him just to come out and tell the truth, but he threatened to kill me if I told anyone. When you came along, and I saw you buddying up to that murdering liar I just couldn't hold it in any longer. You deserve to know the truth."

"If anyone here is a liar it's you Trick," at this moment I hate this man who put a seed of doubt in my mind about the only family I have left here on this Earth. I run back to The Hut and decide to confront my dad about this. I have to find out the truth.

I run into my dad's office, out of breath. He and the General were laughing over a few drinks. I guess they both sensed what I had to say was important, so my dad tightly asked, "General, would you mind giving us a minute?" The General slowly stands and walks out the door. "Justin, what's the matter?"

"Is it true? Did you kill Mom?" I barely choked those words out and when they reached my father's ears his face completely drained of color.

"Now, now let's not get too excited. Who told you that?" before I could say anything he answered himself. "What a stupid question. I know who told you. That traitorous idiot Trick. I swore to him that if he told a soul, I'd kill him." My mouth drops, my own father really did kill my mother. Suddenly I can't move, paralyzed by the utter despair of finding out my dad is a murderer.

"General," he screams with spit flying from his mouth. The general opens the door making me realize he must've heard all of that. "Bring Trick to me. It seems he's been slandering his own leader and you know the penalty for treason." My dad turns to me, his voice eerily calm now. "Justin, you're about to see what happens to people who try and cross me."

I'm still paralyzed, but my brain is not. Every second I am thinking a hundred different things. How did this man who used to take me sailing every week, who used to hold me on his shoulders, who used to kiss my mother turn into the monster in front of me today? How did this normal day turn upside down within a matter of minutes?

With my mouth still dropped open in shock, the General returns and throws Trick into the office then steps out and shuts the door. Trick, the once intimidating man, is now on his knees with his hands tied behind him. He looks at me with sadness in his eyes, but no malice is in his voice when he says, "I had to tell you, Justin. I had to tell someone." He begins speaking to my father, "You don't deserve to lead. These people trust you. How can you lie to them every day like it's nothing?"

My father opens one of his desk's drawers pulling out a long serrated knife. "Trick, it *is* nothing. I am the best leader for these hopeless people. Without me, they'd all be dead. Just like you're about to be." To my horror, he throws the knife across the room. A loud thud echoes on the wall as the blade buries itself into Tricks chest. Blood trickles down his yellow shirt and he falls to his side, arms still tied behind his back. I fall to my knees and watch as he twitches in pain, his eyes slowly glazing over.

He's dead.

I look at my father's calm face, and it makes me sick. He spits out, "Son if you are like Trick and have any stupid convictions in your heart, I suggest you keep them to yourself." The General comes back in and begins dragging out Trick like nothing happened.

"You can leave now Justin."

I walk out of the room in a haze, not able to process what just happened. The General steps back in the office leaving the door open. I stop to overhear my dad, "General, my son knows too much. We've got to get rid of him, quickly but also in the right way. Why don't we let him run for a bit then tell the community he killed Trick for power? As you know the punishment for treason and murder is death," my dad laughs mechanically. "When the community sees me kill my own son in the name of our laws they will have no doubt that I'm loyal to being their leader."

I feel like throwing up. I've got to get away from here.

18. Running

As I run down the silvery street, I know that I can't leave without saying goodbye to Anne before escaping. It may end up costing my life, but she has to know how much she means to me. I soon run through Doc's door and lock it behind me. I see Anne sitting at the kitchen table reading and Doc standing over the stove top making what smells like fish.

ANNE'S PERSPECTIVE

I was just getting to the good part of my book when Justin runs through our door at full speed. I stand up so fast my chair falls backward, "Justin? What's happened, are you alright?" Dad turns off the stove with a worried look on his face.

In between breaths, he says, "Trick... Trick is dead. My dad just killed him, and he killed my mother too. He's going to pin it all on me. I have to get out of here." He is speaking so fast I can barely understand, but when my brain catches up with my ears, I'm stunned.

"Whoa there, slow down. Everything's gonna be okay." My dad says while I rub Justin's back trying to soothe him. "Your dad killed Trick, and he is planning to blame you?"

Justin nods his head yes, "He wants to kill me because of what I know about my mom. He's insane, and he *will* kill me if I don't leave now." His fingers run through my hair, "I just had to come and tell you Anne that I... I lo...," I have to stop him right there. Now that I've known him I feel that if he left, my world would not be as bright. Colors would dull, the sky would lose its' mystery, and I'd never get to see him again. That makes my decision easy.

Determinedly I tell my dad and Justin, "Don't say anything else. You don't have to say goodbye because I'm coming with you." I look at my father and see sadness in his eyes but also understanding.

JUSTIN'S PERSPECTIVE

My entire being wants to give into what she's saying, but instead of telling her that, I have to say, "Anne, no. It is too dangerous out there, and I can't take you away from your dad, your home."

"But you wouldn't be taking me away; I'd be going of my own free will." She looks at Doc with a look that seemed to say 'back me up here.'

Doc surprises me by bravely saying, "Justin I think you should both go. Anne, I would do the same thing for your mother and if you love this boy like you say you do no matter what happens the only thing that will matter is that you're with him."

A loud noise seeps into the walls and snaps our attention outside. Doc peeks out of the window blinds, "Looks like it's all the guards in the community and they're headed up our walkway. Justin get in here and don't make a sound," Doc firmly pushes me into a small closet underneath the stairs. "Anne go to your room and start packing up anything that you need."

I hear a knock at the door and the sound of Doc opening it. The General speaks first "Doc we've just discovered that Justin Price has murdered Trick. He is very dangerous, and we need to find him before he hurts anyone else."

Doc answers with a stunning ability to act shocked, "That's awful I will surely keep an eye out for him."

"Make sure you do. Everyone knows he's got a fancy for Anne so make sure that she's safe until we find him." The door closes, and I slowly open the closet. Anne runs down the stairs, a bag in hand.

"Okay you two, there's not much time for goodbye. Justin take good care of my girl." He goes to Anne and embraces her in a hug, "Anne, my darling Anne, I'm so proud of you. I will miss you every day, but the knowledge that you will be happy is enough for me." Tears slide down Doc's cheeks as he caresses Anne's face and embraces her in another hug. "Now go! There's a truck in the backyard that should work just fine. I'll lead the guards in the opposite direction. When I say the word 'Hurry,' gun that truck as fast as it will go and you get out of here."

Once in the truck I reach for Anne's hand and hold on tightly. She whispers, "We'll be alright. Just pretend we're going on a drive." I have a feeling she's trying to convince herself more than me. "Look there's my dad." I look to where she pointed, and sure enough Doc is waving his arms to get the guards attention. We hear him yell, "There they go! He has Anne. Please HURRY and stop them." I flip on the beige truck and press the accelerator so hard the tires spin for one moment. Then, we are jerked backward as the force of the truck propels forward.

In the rearview mirror, I see the guards and Doc running in the opposite direction, but someone else is there too. Corwin. He isn't with the others. He's looking straight at the runaway truck. I fear he is going to alert the small army that is looking for us, but he doesn't. I silently thank God and ram straight through the closed gates. Anne and I both scream; half in fear, half in excitement. The interior of the truck itself seems to seethe with adrenaline.

19. First Kiss and Coincidence

Anne has the idea to stop by the farm and gather some supplies, "Trick was Freddy's friend. Once we tell him what happened I just know he'll help us." she reasons.

I pull into the gravel driveway, and we both jump out and start looking for Freddy. I mean Fred, I correct myself after remembering the time I first met him. He was in the barn when we run in; stepping on a few chicken in the process. "Anne, what is going on. You look like you're running from the devil himself."

"That's because we are running from the devil. The Leader killed Trick. I'm sorry to tell you like this. I know he was your friend." Anne says sympathetically.

Fred looks down at his muddy boots, "Trick

warned me something like this would happen. He told me all about the Leader killing his wife and threatening to kill Trick if he told anyone. Last few days I noticed him getting antsy about keeping it a secret anymore. He never was one to keep his mouth shut."

I've been keeping watch at the barn door, and in the distance I see a cloud of dust forming on the horizon. "Anne. Their coming, fast."

Anne impresses me by keeping her voice level, "Freddy, I know you need time to process all this, but we need your help."

Within two minutes Fred's team of farmers had our truck loaded with every kind of food they grow as well as a couple gallons of water. Watching how much these farmers respect him, I think he should be the community's leader and not my lying, murdering father. Maybe he can lead a revolution against my father and his puppet, the General.

Anne hugs Fred goodbye and gets in the truck. I want to say something, but instead, Fred puts out his hand for me to shake, "You can call me Freddy." I grin and run back to the truck.

Once we are out of the driveway, the cloud of dust seems to have gotten a lot closer. My palms are sweating, and Anne keeps turning around, paranoid that they will catch us. Anne excitedly gets me to look behind us, "Look Justin. Freddy and the farmers are making a road block!" Sure enough, in the rearview mirror, I see all the farmers have created a line across the road. The three cars following us screech to a halt. When they stop, I push this truck faster than I thought it could go. We soon lose sight of the farm as we dip behind a hill.

Anne sighs in relief, "I think we can actually get away. Wow, I never would've believed it, but here we are."

"Your confidence in me is inspiring," I joke, but then turn more serious, "Anne thank you for coming with me. I know it wasn't an easy thing to do, but I am so happy that you're here. I feel as if I have a reason to live when I'm with you." She leans over and brushes her lips on the corner of my mouth. I feel my face turning red and the goofy grin that only comes when Anne is around spreads across my face.

We drive for hours, but it feels like minutes. Anne's contagious laugh fills the air like the warmth of the sun, even though it is completely dark outside. With the feeling of the wheel on my hands and the pressure of the pedal on my foot, I realized how much I'd missed driving. With Anne by my side, I love it even more. I've been enjoying myself so much I haven't kept my eye on the solar energy gauge. The truck begins to sputter forward slowly as it switches to its backup battery. "We need to find somewhere to park until morning," I say.

Anne points to a large bush just big enough to fit a car behind a little way off the road, "We could pull behind there. It'd offer us some camouflage so that if anyone comes by there'd be a lesser chance of being seen." I agree and steer the slow moving vehicle behind the bush.

With both of our seats laid back, we look through the sunroof at the twinkling stars. We are silent for a bit until Anne ask, "Can you tell me something you've never told anyone before?"

I think back through my life and decide to tell her about the man that saved my life a few years ago. "I went through depression when I got out of college, and it got so bad that I wanted to kill myself," Anne tenderly picks up my hand with kindness on her moonlit face. "Before I could do anything drastic God sent me a pastor to save me just at the right moment."

I look over at her expecting to see judgment on her face but instead I see respect, "That's a difficult thing to come back from. I'm thankful for that pastor. You know my grandfather was a pastor, and he always said that most people could be helped by simply listening to them. I haven't seen him in a long time. He lived all the way in Florida. I don't even know if he heard about Mom."

I look at her for a long time with curiosity, "Florida was where I met the pastor that took me in. What was your grandfather's name?"

"William Barrios. I think I packed a picture of him somewhere," she reaches for her bag and starts to rifle through her things. I'm in shock. There is no way it's the same guy. That'd be too much of a coincidence. There's no way she is the granddaughter of the man who saved my life.

Anne hands me an old fashioned picture, and as I

hold it closer to the sunroof, the Pastor Barrios that I remember comes to focus, "This is the same pastor that I know Anne. This man, your grandfather, changed my life."

She looks at me with wide eyes, "You're just kidding, right? If you were telling the truth, that'd be too crazy."

"I promise that I am not lying," I pause to check the photo one more time. It really is him, "What are the chances that your grandfather, who lives across the country, saves my life and I end up here falling in love with his granddaughter." I realize that I had let the 'L' word slip from my lips, but I don't regret it.

ANNE'S PERSPECTIVE

My grandfather that I haven't seen in so long saved Justin. If I didn't know that God can do anything, there's no way I'd believe this. Just as my mind is trying to process this incredible new information I hear Justin say that he is falling in love with me. My heart skips a beat. He's falling in love with me? The past few weeks of being around him surface in my memories. I gaze into his deep

134

brown eyes and tell him the truth, "I'm falling in love with you too." We both lean closer to each other, and our lips meet. A burst of electricity fills the universe and light explodes all around us.

As this one perfect moment ends, we realize that the light that had erupted around us was coming from headlights of other cars.

20. The Fishery

Justin and I immediately shrink down, attempting invisibility. I peek out of the passenger seat window to find three of the community cars shining their headlights right on us. I can only pray that the bush is enough to hide any glinting metal of the truck. I've lived in the community for over two years, and that's long enough to know that if they captured us, Justin would be killed.

The light starts to get brighter as it moves toward us, but then the three cars begin to reverse. "I am pretty sure they're turning around," I whisper.

Sure enough, their lights slowly fade, leaving us once again in moonlit darkness. I hear Justin adjust his seat to a sitting position, "Thank goodness. What are the odds of them turning around right here? I'm just glad they seem to have given up the search." I smile in agreement, and then I yawn. I had forgotten how exhausted I am. Justin says "Why don't you get some sleep I'll stay up and keep watch."

I decide not to argue, "Thanks, just make sure you wake me for my turn." I lay my seat all the way back and when my eyes close I am asleep.

Sunlight warms my face, slowly waking me. I stretch my arm toward the sunroof that now lets in the sun, instead of the moon. I look over to Justin and see he is sleeping peacefully. I softly shake him awake. He tries to open his eyes, but his eyelids only get halfway up. I laugh quietly, "Good morning."

"Good morning, actually, great morning because I get to see you." he leans over the console, and we have our second kiss.

Stepping outside the truck my tennis shoes hit the rocky sand and when I walk back to grab breakfast, puffs of dust follow my steps. "Thank goodness Freddy was able to stock us up before we left," I say while grabbing an orange.

"Yeah, last time I was stuck out in the desert we only had cactus to help us out. I think I still have some needles in my hand," after passing me a water Justin examines his hand as if expecting to see remnants of cactus there.

"I don't think I'd like cactus," we stand in silence for a moment watching the sun rise into the sky like a balloon released to the heavens. I break the silence, "Alright, what is our next plan?"

"I was thinking last night that if we continue down this highway, we might end up somewhere we can stay for a bit. Just until we can figure out everything." That sounded good to me, and soon we are headed back down the road.

JUSTIN'S PERSPECTIVE

Driving for about two hours with nothing but desert to look at, can only be made enjoyable by Anne. Her stories and off-key singing cause me to hope this road goes on forever, but all things come to an end eventually. Desert slowly switches to beat up houses and the smell of salty air. "We must be near the ocean," Anne crinkles her nose as the smell of fish trickles into the truck. As we keep driving forward, Anne is proved right. At the end of the small ghost town is a dilapidated dock with a large wooden building to the side that has the words

MEL'S FISHERY

painted in large letters. The ocean rises and falls causing the few boats left tied to the dock to sway back and forth. Only the one closest to the wooden fishery looked seaworthy, "Why would people leave their boats?" Anne asks.

We are still sitting in the truck as I peer more closely at the vessels, "I think those are manual boats. I guess their owners didn't feel like dragging them out of California. Wow, they must be almost fifty years old. When I was still living in South Carolina, my family had a boat similar to these. Of course, it was a bit smaller." I flip off the truck and open the door. Anne does the same and starts to walk toward the docks.

A man's voice yells out from the nicer boat, "Derek, did you hear somethin'?" I quickly pull Anne behind some stacked crates.

"No, Ron I didn't. Now shut-up and let me go back to sleep. No one's been in this town since we got here and there sure ain't no boogeyman around." the guy named Derek viciously yells back.

"Let's get back to the truck," I say to Anne. We run low to the ground and quietly climb into our vehicle. Anne and I both cringe as the engine starts back up, but the man on the boat doesn't seem to hear us. Past the fishery I see rain clouds beginning to form. We need to find shelter and fast unless we want our food supplies to be drenched.

Driving past the tired looking houses I see one with an open garage attached to the side; I back the truck into the empty space as the heavy gray clouds cause rain to thrum loudly on the garage roof, "We got here just in time. One minute longer and all our food would have been sitting in water," Anne pauses, "I think we should stay here until morning. How about you?"

"We might not have another choice. This rain looks like it could go on forever," I say solemnly. Seeing that fishery and the old boats reminded me of two things; Jay and my hometown.

Anne could tell I needed some time to think so she kisses my cheek and opens the truck door, "I'm going to take a look around this house. I'll be back soon," she closes the truck, and her golden ponytail disappears behind the house's unlocked door. I can't help but smile at her curiosity and suddenly the fierce desire to give her a normal life falls on my heart like a two-ton weight. Jay's voice echoes in my memories, "Justin, you're here for a reason." What if the reason is to get Anne back to the real world? This idea randomly popped into my head like a wound up jack-in-the-box. It was one of those ideas that you know is crazy, but it overtakes your very existence until it has a solution. My brain goes into overdrive trying to figure out how to accomplish- what I believe to be- the reason I am here. When Anne gets back into the truck carrying two blankets, I get ready to introduce her to my idea.

As I take the musty blanket, she offers me I say, "You deserve better than scavenging empty houses for holey blankets."

She shakes out her blanket before getting back in the truck, "What do you mean? Scavenging is the only way we can survive, it's not like there are any home decor shops to visit," she says brushing off my comment.

"Anne, what if I told you we could escape this prison world?"

"I'd say you're crazy because there's no way to break out of the wall. I remember seeing it be built, Justin. They dug twenty feet down and poured concrete so no one could dig themselves out, officials are posted all along the wall, particularly at the ends so no one can go around it. There's no way to climb it. There is no way to escape," her grey eyes shine with tears, or maybe it's the reflection of the rain.

I fully turn towards her making my voice as serious as possible, "We may can't dig under, climb over, or get around the wall, but we can float away from it."

ANNE'S PERSPECTIVE

Justin seems so excited, but I know better than to get my hopes up. "Where did this come from? Look I realize that you're probably thinking a lot about your friend from seeing the fishery back at the docks and if my dad turned out to be a homicidal maniac I'd be thinking of crazy ideas too, but the truth is that this is our lives now."

He's crestfallen for just a moment but then his

face lights up again, "Just hear me out. That boat we saw today, with the guys on it, I know how to sail it, and I know that we'd eventually reach land; land that isn't filled with murderous criminals. I could get us out of here," he has my hands in his now, and his hopeful eyes look into mine.

I want to give in, but the practical side of my brain takes over, "Justin, you have no idea how much I want to get back to really living instead of just surviving, but there are so many things that could go wrong. What if officials patrol the ocean, what if we sink, or never find land? Plus, I can't imagine that the government would've let anyone leave a usable boat behind the wall."

He pauses, putting two fingers on his temple like he always does when he is thinking super hard, "You're right, there are risks, but if we succeeded wouldn't the reward out pay the risks? That boat those guys were on today looked solid, and I doubt the government considered old manual boats as usable since only a few people know how to use them. If we could somehow commandeer the boat and load it with our supplies, we could sail away to freedom." I look outside, watching the steady rainfall. He really thinks this is possible. What if it is? I allow myself to imagine a life back in the real world. We could get married in a beautiful church, buy a house, go through all the ups and downs that life lived in freedom brings. I want that so badly my heart begins to hurt. My realistic side tells me I'd have a better chance of surviving if I stayed here in California, but the hopeful and courageous side brings up images of what my future would look like outside of this Prison Wall. I could have the life I had always dreamed of when I was a kid. A quote I read once sticks in my head, 'At the end of the day, we must go forward with hope, and not backward with fear.' Whoever said that was right; I can't run away from my dream life because of fear.

Eventually, I turn back to Justin with my mind made up, "Okay, I'm in. Now how are we going to get those guys off that boat?"

21. Fish Nets

We stayed up most of the night trying to figure out a plan. After two hours of brainstorming, I felt like my mind was one of those old, slow computers called laptops. We haven't been able to think of any plan yet, but at least we both agreed that we should trap the two guys in the fishery; neither of us could imagine killing them in cold blood. Now we just have to figure out *how* to trap them. I ask Justin, "Do you know anything about fisheries? Did you have one in your hometown?"

Justin shakes his head no, "We only had one boat dock. The only thing I know about fisheries is what my friend Jay told me about when he worked at one."

I faintly remember one lunch conversation where Justin told me about his friend Jay, but I had forgotten he worked at a fishery, "Maybe he said something that would be helpful! Think really hard. What do you remember?" I grin as he immediately touches his temple.

"Wait a minute; I remember him telling me some story about how one guy got trapped under a really heavy fishnet." I motion with my hand for him to keep talking, "If we could find a net like that and somehow drop it on those guys we'd have time to load up the boat before they got out."

"That's a good plan, but it isn't full-proof. We have to make sure there even is a net. Then, we've got to hang it somehow on the ceiling and then get those guys under it."

"How about we scope out the fishery really early tomorrow morning and figure out all the details then?"

My mouth opens in a yawn that makes my eyes burn with fatigue, "Maybe we shouldn't scope it out *really* early in the morning," Justin chuckles in amusement, I lightly punch his arm because I truly am serious about not waking up early.

22. The Trap

The next morning, Justin has to literally drag me out of the car and onto my feet, "Oh come on! The sun isn't even awake yet." I sleepily argue.

"I know, but I want to get the trap set up before noon. By the way, even though you look really tired, I still think you're gorgeous," He gives me a kiss, and I roll my eyes with an inerasable smile painted on my face.

As we walk to the docks, the grayish early morning is crisp and refreshing. Soon the outline of the fishery comes into view. We search the perimeter and finally find a door that had been bordered up with planks of wood. Justin and I begin to pull off the wood, getting a few splinters in the process. Inside the worn wooden walls is about twenty concrete boxes. Ten are lined up on one side and the other ten on the opposite. The smell of rotting fish almost makes me almost lose my breakfast. Every box was filled to the brim with repulsive green water. Holding our noses, we walked through the place. Decaying fish lay stagnant on top of the green sludge water, flies feed on the putrid flesh, "This is horrible. Please tell me you see a net?" I almost take my hand of my nose to laugh at Justin's nasally voice, but I stop myself just in time. Instead, I take a good stock of our foul surroundings. My eyes catch something rope-like behind one of the boxes. We go over and find the net that we will use for a trap.

We both run outside, crunching over as we gulp in the fresh air with indulgent breaths. "Luckily, there's a pulley hook right above that net. If we can stand going back in there and pulling the net up, we'll have our trap set," Justin says while standing straight again.

"If you take care of that I'll look around the place and see if there is anything that could be helpful on our upcoming cruise." Obviously, I am joking about the whole 'cruise' part, but I like making Justin laugh. Hopefully this journey will be more like a cruise than anything else.

"Good idea. There's an office room in the back. If

you can, try and check that too." I nod, pinch my nose again and bravely walk back inside.

Justin goes straight to the net and begins fussing with the hook hanging from the ceiling. I on the other hand head straight past the fishy graves and into the office room. I have to kick the door a couple of times for it to pop open. Inside smells musty like it hasn't been inhabited for a while. The layer of dust over everything confirms my suspicion.

All I see is a bunch of rusted metal and an old desk with nothing on it. I start to open all of the drawers to find more rusty metal. In the last drawer, I see something silver buried under old rags that, of course, have a smell of fish. It's small enough to fit in my hand, and there are a couple of buttons and me being me, I immediately press the big red one. Light flickers in front of me and a holographic image appears. It's a map! There is a small blue dot that represents the device's current location. This will definitely help us out in the ocean, where the only point of reference to guide you is the sun and waves.

I walk out of the office and back into the main section of the fishery and take one more look around. I wave at Justin who is across the room. He waves for me to follow him as he quickly moves toward the exit.

Once again we are outside gulping for oxygen. I show Justin the map device, "This is great. See that blue dot? That is where we are and if we zoom out," Justin presses one of the other buttons, "we can decide where we want to go. I am thinking these islands right here." He points to a group of islands south of California.

"Is there anything closer? That just looks like a lot of ocean between us and those green dots." I say nervously.

"Honestly, I think that will be our best bet," Justin says turning off the map.

"Well, we still have to actually get the boat," I say, reminding him.

"Geez, I almost forgot that part," he says sarcastically. Then he gets serious again, "I got the hook and the net ready. Now all we have to do is figure out how we're going to get those criminals where we want them."

I think for a minute and then an idea hits me that I know Justin is not going to like, "All we need is to get them right under the net and drop it, right? Let me get their attention so they'll chase me inside the building. When I get them in the right spot you drop the net right on top of them."

Justin frowns, immediately showing dislike of my plan, "Anne, there's way too many things that could go wrong. Those guys could have guns, or you could fall and break your leg. It's too dangerous."

"I'm not that clumsy, nor do I need protecting," I say defensively. "Look, I know enough about sailing to know that there's only a small window of time during the year to travel somewhat safely on the ocean. Every hour we waste on land makes it that much more dangerous for us out there," I point toward the rolling ocean, "You know I'm right and unless you can think of another idea, like, right now, we need to use my plan. Let me be the bait. I can do this."

"I know you can, I just don't want you to have to," he replies. I appreciate him wanting to protect me, but I'm not some fragile butterfly that has to be handled with care. I'm strong and capable of doing anything, especially leading a couple of meatheads into a building.

I give him a hug and whisper in his ear, "Everything will turn out just fine, you'll see. And by the end of the day, we will be sailing to freedom.

The sun beats down on my shoulders as I wait behind a rusted machine. I have to get the boat guys attention soon. Justin is in the fishery waiting for me to run them under the net so he can cut the hook; trapping them underneath four-hundred pounds of damp woven rope.

I see the man named Ron walk out onto the deck, his friend Derek follows. Here we go. I take a deep breath and start screaming, "Help! Help! Please, my boyfriend is hurt." I point to the fishery.

Both men almost jump out their socks in surprise. Ron's face morphs into the creepiest smile I've ever seen, "Well, well, well. What do we got here? Hey missy, we'll come to help you. Just stay right there," they started moving toward me, licking their lips like wolves stalking a deer. I doubt their thinking about helping me, but in a minute they're the ones who will need help.

I begin running across the dockyard to the fishery.

I look behind me to make sure they're chasing me. They are. The guy named Derek was lagging behind because of the fat that droops over his pants, but Ron seemed to be getting closer. I pick up my speed.

My lungs take one deep breath before plunging in the dark and dank fishery. I look up and quickly find the net hanging from the ceiling ready to trap my pursuers. My feet automatically take me under the net, then turn me around to face the two criminals. Even in the dim light, I can see their red tattoos burning like fire, "Please my boyfriend is right over here. If you don't help me, he'll die."

Derek, who is breathing heavily, chokes out, "Honey, I think you'd be better off without a boyfriend. We'll take care of you jus' fine."

They begin to advance toward me, and I step back a few feet. When they reach the spot under the net, I yell, "Now Justin!"

A loud zipping noise rings through the foul air as the net is released, followed by a thud and the terrified screams of two disgusting men. The sunlight slants in through a hole in the roof as I see how well our little trap

153

worked. The wet rope weighs the two figures down as they struggle in confusion.

"What's going on? Get this thing off us! It feels like it's crushing my ribs." Ron flails under the roped net.

I see them wriggling under the weight of our trap. I spit out, "Boys we need your boat. You're lucky we didn't decide to kill you." Justin grabs my hand and pulls me outside. I can still hear the two guys bickering while trying to lift off the massive net.

"Anne, that was incredible! You're incredible. I thought for sure I'd have to jump out and beat some people up." Justin says cracking his knuckles like a tough guy. He put his arm around me, and we make the long trek back to the truck.

Once we drive the truck back to the docks, Justin begins looking over the boat to make sure it is actually seaworthy while I start loading our supplies.

JUSTIN'S PERSPECTIVE

When I first step foot on the boat, memories of my childhood come flooding back. Memories of my dad and I casting out fishing lines and talking all day are now tainted by the knowledge that he killed Mom. I sigh, turning my attention back to the integrity of the boat. The top deck seems to be in great shape, but the mechanics down below are what I'm worried about.

I find the trapdoor that leads down to the solar powered engine and gears. Once I step down to the pitch-black underbelly of our boat, I fumble around to find the light switch. When my hand finally flips the switch, uncovered light bulbs glow an eerie yellow, and by that light, I begin my inspection. After about twenty minutes of meticulously going over every gear, plug, and bolt I head back up to the cabin to tell Anne the verdict.

23. Setting Sail

I poke my head out of the trapdoor just as Anne is setting down the last water container. She smiles and asks hopefully, "Hey you. How does everything look?"

I grab a rag that lay on the captain's chair and start cleaning up my greasy hands, "I am excited to announce that we are ready to set sail. Whoever had this boat before those two doofuses in the fishery took super good care of this old thing." I say while patting the wall of the boat's cabin.

"That's wonderful news. I have some good news too. I found a fishing rod, and I put it out on the dock We can get fish if our food supplies start to run out. How many weeks do you think this stuff we already have will last us?" she asks, kicking a box of vegetables to her right.

I do some calculations in my head. If we drink one gallon of water a day between the both of us and we have twenty gallons, "The water should last us twenty days, thirty tops if we ration it. The food won't last as long, but we have that fishing rod that we can use. The map we found in the fishery shows we can make it to those islands in about twenty-five days if the wind is on our side."

"I've only been on one boat in my life, and I was six. I really hope I'm not prone to seasickness." Anne laughs nervously.

I love how she tries to make every situation light, but I can tell she is thinking about everything that could go wrong. I jump off the truck bed and embrace her, kissing the top of her head, "We're going to be okay. You've got the best sailor in the world right here."

Anne smiles at my confidence, "I guess the only way to prove that is to start sailing. I'll check the truck one more time for anything else we could use, and you get us ready to leave the docks."

I double check the boat for any cracks, leaks, or engine trouble. Thankfully, this manual boat is run off solar power like most vehicles and doesn't have any fatal wear-and-tear. I get back up to the cabin and stand behind the captain's controls. Anne is sitting at the bow looking out to the setting sun. I say a silent prayer and start the boat's engine. The purr of the mechanics reverberates throughout the port yard. Anne looks back at me, and I give her a thumbs up. I press the throttle, and we begin pulling away from the old dock.

The memories I have of growing up on the ocean soon come back to me. By the time the sun is completely hidden by the straight line of the horizon, I could drive this boat in my sleep. Anne is with me in the cabin now. She curiously points to every button and lever asking me to tell her how it works. Once we've been through everything, I ask her, "You want to take over?"

She apprehensively says, "I can try. Maybe when I get the hang of it, you can get some sleep."

"That'd be amazing. Just put your hand on the wheel, yep that's right, and the lever here controls our speed. If the waves get any bigger slow way down and just let the currents take us, even if we start getting a bit off course."

"Got it. Hey, this is fun!" I smile because she's smiling. About an hour later Anne looks almost more comfortable at the wheel than a seasoned sailor. Once I know that she can handle everything I turn to a cot bolted down in the back of the cabin to get some sleep.

ANNE'S PERSPECTIVE

I've always been impressed by the power and vastness of the ocean, but being in the middle of its wild unpredictability makes me respect the salty water even more. The many flood lights on our boat mix with the bright moonlight to feature the frothy white waves that never stop moving. I turn to see Justin fast asleep with his arm slung over the side of the cot. I turn back to the ocean. All there is in front of us, behind us, to the sides of us is water. The shores of California disappeared a long time ago, swallowed up where the sky meets the ocean.

I click on the holographic map to check our course. We still have a long way to travel. Seeing the blinking light on the map that is our boat leaving the shores of California behind gives me a heavy sadness. That has been where I've lived my entire life. That's where my mom is buried; where I left my dad. Suddenly the vastness of the ocean makes me feel a loneliness that devours all my energy.

I step away from the controls to wake Justin. He slowly comes back to consciousness, "I'm getting tired. Do you mind taking over?" I ask him trying my best to keep the sadness out of my voice.

"Not at all." He seems to sense my loneliness, "Do you want to talk?"

I put on a small smile at the tender concern in his voice, "Maybe in the morning. I'm just missing my dad, but I'll feel better when I get some sleep. It's been a long day."

He nods in agreement, "You're right about that. I can't believe it was only this morning that we snared those creeps." He quietly sits beside me on the cot for a few moments, "Anne I am so sorry that I am the reason you left your dad. I can't imagine what you're going through and I want to do everything I can to make this easier if that's even possible. I promise that the rest of my life will be dedicated to making it up to you."

Justin's guilt pierces my heart. I have to make sure

he understands that I don't blame him for anything, "You have nothing to make up to me. I left my dad of my own free will because I knew that a world without you wouldn't be worth living in. We've known each other for a few months now and this time has been the happiest of my life. Dad understood that, and I will always have him in my memory, just like I have my mom." I said all that to soothe Justin's mind, but I actually made myself feel better too.

Justin's lips softly touch mine and his nose brushes the side of my face. When he pulls away, I can see a mix of many emotions in his brown eyes. The butterflies in my stomach start to flutter again, "Good night Anne. I'll see you in the morning," As I lay down he takes off his jacket and places it over me like a blanket. He gives me one more kiss on my forehead and walks toward the control table.

24. Depleted Supplies

<u>ANNE'S PERSPECTIVE</u>

We've been sailing for two weeks.

That's fourteen days.

I'm going out of my mind.

The map shows that we are about ten days away from the islands that we want to reach, but we only have enough food and water for *two* more days. Justin tried to catch a fish, but it was so heavy that the fishing pole snapped in half. Now we have no way of getting more food. I can't even say what happened to our water supplies. We are down to one gallon. It's like the air itself evaporated our only source of life. I am trying so hard to be strong and not show Justin how scared I am, but my mask is cracking. I don't want to die.

JUSTIN'S PERSPECTIVE

My head feels like a drummer is beating the inside of my skull. Sunlight cuts through my eyes and seems to give energy to the pounding. I know that I need more water, but we're so low already. I'm trying my best to keep Anne from seeing my worry, but I think she knows that we're in trouble.

After drinking the rationed one sip of water for the evening, Anne comes to me, "Justin, I know you're trying to downplay our situation here, but I'm not blind. We are running out of supplies too fast. I think we should pray for a miracle because that's the only way we are getting off this boat alive."

For the first time since we began this journey, I didn't try to tell her everything would be okay. Instead, we got down on our knees and prayed that God would send us a miracle.

"I'll take the first shift tonight. The waves are looking higher than usual." I say while opening the cabin's door for Anne.

At the wheel I have a good view of the ocean and

what I see makes my heart beat a little faster. The waves are quickly becoming higher than our deck and the sky has taken on a sickly green color. I think we are headed straight into a storm.

25. The Storm

"Anne!" I am using all the strength I have left to hold the wheel steady. Rain is coming horizontally at the cabin window.

The wind is so strong.

Anne screams above the sound of thrashing water, "Oh no, Justin our boat can't take this kind of beating. What are we going-" she is cut short when the very ground underneath us tilts. I hold onto the wheel as my legs fall out from under me. Anne is slammed into the wall of the cabin. Another wave hits and our boat straightens out again. I leave the wheel, crawling over to Anne as my whole world rocks viciously back and forth.

I feel something sticky on the ground.

I hold my hand up in the light provided by the flashing lightning. Red blood glistens back at me. Anne doesn't move when I finally reach her. I check her pulse, "Please God, don't let her be dead. Get us through this." I think I am falling into shock. My fingers find Anne's pulse, and I exhale in relief. The boat is still savagely rocking while I drag myself and Anne to the captain's chair.

I clumsily stand and am barley able to get Anne in the chair and buckled in before another massive wave hits. The world spins around me as I fly through the air. My body hits the hard wall, and I black out.

I have this dream that the boat suddenly stops moving and the rain ceases its' pounding. My mother helps me stand and says, "Justin, come back to me. Justin please." I realize that it isn't my mom's voice; it's Anne's. I foggily open my eyes to see the only girl I will ever love crying on my chest. The rain has stopped, and now the sun shone in through the windows. I must've been out awhile. Somehow she had gotten my unconscious self onto the cot, "That was some storm huh?" I ask, my voice sounding more like a frog croaking.

Anne's tear-stained face snaps up in relief, "Thank God. Don't you ever scare me like that again Justin Price. All I remember is it raining really hard. Then next thing I know, I wake up strapped to that chair," she jabs her thumb behind her pointing to the captain's chair. Anne's luggage contents, as well as our last food supplies, litter the ground.

I stiffly sit up, "This must be what it feels like to be ninety years old." Anne scoffs at my lame attempt at a joke. She grabs my tattooed arm as I start to sway dizzily. I notice a bandage on her left wrist and a bruise on her forehead. Remembering the blood, I saw last night I worriedly touch her arm, "Are you alright? Is it a bad cut? We may have some antibiotics in the first aid kit."

"I've already raided the first aid kit, and it's just a scratch. No big deal." She chuckles at all my questions, "What the really important question is, how far did that storm blow us off course?" Anne walks over to the map that is lying on the ground along with many other of our things. I hope it isn't broken.

She presses the button, and a weak image of the ocean appears in front of us, "That can't be right," I take the map and reset the holographic device. Our boat's position doesn't change. The dot representing our boat shows that we are very close to the group of islands we were initially aiming for, but that's not possible, "Anne, according to this we should be seeing land in about an hour."

"What? That's impossible; we were still ten days away from any land last night. Surely the storm couldn't have blown us that far in such a short amount of time," she says with hopeful disbelief.

I look at her with wide eyes, "If this map is showing us the truth. That storm was the miracle we asked for."

26. An End and a Beginning

The map wasn't lying. About an hour later a fuzzy outline of mountains rises out of the ocean like a mirage. As we sail closer, details of the land begin coming into focus. The greenery of trees, buildings, homes, freedom. Anne and I race out of the cabin to the front bow.

"I can't believe this. Justin, we're going to live. We're free! No more worrying about where our next meal is coming from or if some rogues are going to break in and attack. We're free." Anne breathes out looking at the mountainous land that will become our home.

I take her up in my arms and swing her around enjoying the glorious joy of this moment. We stop spinning, and I move her golden hair away from her face. She laces her hand around my neck, and I kiss her. I kiss her with everything I have because she is everything I need. The touch of her lips, the sound of the ocean lapping against land, pure freedom. This moment is one of those rare moments in life where nothing matters except being.

Soon we reach the island's steel boat dock. Yachts and boat homes float nearby. I look back at the torrent ocean. We've been through a lot. I've been through a lot. Far away from the confines of the wall, I realize that before I was arrested, I had been a naive guy that thought freedom was just being able to do whatever you wanted. I never realized how trapped I was throughout my whole life. I wasn't physically bound, but my soul was trapped by the walls that pushed everyone away. When I fell in love with Anne, it was the first time I became truly free. Ironically, I found my freedom behind the prison wall. The walls around my soul tumbled down and opened my eyes to the truth that real happiness can only come from unconditional faith and loving another more than yourself.

I help Anne down from the boat that had carried us all the way from California and breathed in deep. A holographic sign catches my eye. It reads, "Aloha, welcome to Hawaii." I look at Anne in amazement. She simply smiles, and we begin to find our way off the dock.

Anne reaches for my hand as we walk toward the rest of our lives...